Churches Serving Schools

Churches Serving Schools

Helping churches to support their local schools

David W. Lankshear

The National Society
*Leading Education
with a Christian Purpose*
Church House Publishing

National Society/Church House Publishing
Church House
Great Smith Street
London SW1P 3NZ

ISBN 0 7151 4993 8 2nd edition

First edition published 1996

Second edition published 2002 by National Society
Enterprises Ltd

Cover design by Church House Publishing
Printed in England by Biddles Ltd, Guildford
and King's Lynn

Contents

Acknowledgements

The publisher gratefully acknowledges permission to reproduce copyright material in this book. Every effort has been made to trace and contact copyright holders. If there are any inadvertent omissions we apologize to those concerned and undertake to include suitable acknowledgements in all future editions.

Scripture quotations are taken from *The New Revised Standard Version of the Bible* copyright © 1989 by the Division of Christian Education of the National Council of Churches in the USA. Used by permission. All rights reserved.

The Archbishops' Council of the Church of England: Extracts from *The Alternative Service Book 1980*; *Common Worship: Services and Prayers for the Church of England* (2000) and *Patterns for Worship* (1995) are copyright © The Archbishops' Council of the Church of England and reproduced by permission.

Cambridge University Press: Extracts from *The Book of Common Prayer*, the rights in which are vested in the Crown, are reproduced by permission of the Crown's Patentee, Cambridge University Press.

The Continuum International Publishing Group Ltd: Extract from David Foster, ed., *The Catholic Prayerbook from Downside Abbey*, T&T Clark, 1999, reproduced by permission of the publisher.

Christopher Herbert: Extracts from *Prayers for Children* and *Pocket Prayers*, both The National Society/Church House Publishing, 1993 are copyright © Christopher Herbert and reproduced by permission.

Introduction

This book is for all involved in local ministry in the Christian churches. It provides a guide to the schools in the education system of England and Wales and contains a range of suggestions on the ways in which good relations may be developed between churches and the schools in the area that they serve.

The publication of the first edition of this book in 1996 produced a steady flow of responses from people involved in church life, many of which cried out to be incorporated in any new edition. During the period that the book has been in use a number of developments have taken place in education and in churches' thinking about education that have created the need to revisit and expand the text.

One of these developments has been the growing understanding of the importance of the Christian vocation to teach. The Church of England report *The Way ahead*[1] has drawn attention to the need to ensure that we not only present the challenge to teach as an expression of Christian discipleship to every generation but that we also take steps to sustain and develop Christian teachers in their professionalism and in their faith. This report is so important to the Anglican Church that most chapters of this book now begin with a quotation from its recommendations.

A second development has been the reforms in education that have been implemented since the first publication of *Churches Serving Schools*. The most obvious of these has been the demise of grant maintained schools and the advent of foundation schools.

What has emerged from the process of review and revision in the light of these developments is an entirely new text. This is offered in order to help all Christian churches reflect on their current practice and develop their work to support teachers and to support local schools. A new section on the National Society's web site contains supplementary material, useful resources and the pages of this book, which churches may wish to use as resources for worship, prayer or discussion. No individual can possibly do everything suggested in these pages. No church will need to do it all, but every church should be addressing some, at least, of the issues raised.

I am grateful to my colleagues within the staff of the Board of Education and National Society for their contributions to and comments on this new text. In particular, my thanks are due to Alison Seaman and Colin Hopkins for their contributions and to Pat Barton and Julia Jones for sorting out the notes, comments and loose pieces of paper and converting them into a coherent text.

Part 1

An urgent task:
why churches should serve schools

1 *Why should churches serve teachers?*

> Through the Dioceses, all parishes should be urged, not just
> once but repeatedly, to put before people what it means to
> be a Christian teacher and, in appropriate cases, encourage
> the vocation to teach.
>
> Education Sunday should be celebrated in all parishes and
> the service should actively involve Christian teachers.
>
> Recommendations from *The Way ahead*

Oh, you are a teacher, what do you teach?

Teachers[2] are familiar with that question. Some teachers answer by naming a subject or curriculum area; others respond by interpreting the 'what' as a 'who' and indicating the age group of their class. This usually stops the conversation, particularly if the answer involves young children. The more interesting and important question is

Why do you teach?

It may receive rather different answers if asked in the moments after a good set of test results are announced or on the third consecutive wet lunch hour in November in an inner city primary school.

Professionally the answer is crucial. Research shows that effective teachers have a clear understanding of their personal answer to the question and that this underpins everything that they do (see for example the report on effective teachers by Hay McBer, 2000).

Some teachers will provide an answer to this question that relates their professional task to their religious faith. Many, but not all, of such teachers will be Christian. The Anglican report *The Way ahead* identifies the need for Christian teachers to be at work in all schools, but particularly in schools that have a 'religious character' (see page 101).

Most Christian churches share the understanding that Christian teachers are needed for work in all types of schools in England and Wales. From this shared understanding a number of questions follow:

- How do Christians become teachers?

- How do Christians who are teachers become Christian teachers?

- What helps Christian teachers to grow in their faith and in their profession?

Every church should reflect on these questions and consider what it might be able to contribute to the processes involved.

Importance of the work

> The gifts he gave were that some would be apostles, some prophets, some evangelists, some pastors and teachers, to equip the saints for the work of ministry.
>
> Ephesians 4.11-12

Many teachers regard such texts as personally important, because they understand Paul's words as affirming that their gifts come from the Spirit. Their sense of vocation is therefore affirmed.

> I came that they may have life, and have it abundantly.
>
> John 10.10

The education that takes place in school can, at its best, be life changing and life enhancing. It provides young people with the tools for learning and living and contributes to the priceless gift of life lived more abundantly (see the quotation above). These fine words are a long way from the feelings experienced while doing playground duty on a dark February morning. For all teachers there must be a balance struck between the reality of the 'February morning' feeling and the vision of the task and its importance. Too often the 'reality' of the February morning dominates.

Recently I was enduring one of these spells when 'February morning' was the dominant feeling. After church one of the congregation came up to me and said,

'Are you all right'? I mumbled something in reply. She said, 'Look after yourself, you're a very special person.' 'February morning' suddenly retreated in that simple moment of someone asserting their view of my value as a human being, perhaps as a professional.

This understanding of value and self-worth is important for teachers. Teaching is a profession. With any profession there is knowledge you have to acquire, skills you must develop and practise, and experience, judgement and wisdom you must seek to obtain. There are professional disciplines you must acquire, including managing your time so that the hours outside the classroom sustain those within it. There are professional attributes such as the ability to control a class of children but they are not in themselves sufficient to practise effectively as a good teacher. To be a good teacher requires much more than skill, it includes an element of performance. It has something of a performing art about it. To perform well, consistently, you have to feel good about what you are doing and you must have confidence in your role. This is why 'teacher morale' is so important. This is why society in general and churches in particular should be encouraging and supporting teachers.

Basically, if you are feeling like Eeyore on a bad day it is hard to be a combination of Pooh, Tigger and Christopher Robin in the classroom.

Summary

This chapter has set out to explore some of the reasons why local churches should support all teachers, but particularly those teachers who are also Christians and Christian teachers in their congregations and in their local schools. A footnote to the chapter heading drew attention to the obvious fact that most churches will want to include in their understanding of 'teachers' all those who work in or serve the schools.

It is accepted that a similar case could be made for the support of health or caring professions and of Christians in their many occupations. Some of the ideas in this chapter, if adopted, would achieve that support. This is a book about education and the ways in which churches can support teachers and schools however, and so there is no reason why there should be an apology for the special pleading that says that churches should find ways to support and serve teachers.

2   Why should churches serve schools?

Parishes and schools should pray regularly for each other.

Recommendation from *The Way ahead*

There are many possible answers to the question posed by the title of this chapter. Sometimes the question is phrased in terms of priorities as in this quotation from the elderly childless church council member.

> I don't know why our priest spends so much time in that school. If he didn't keep popping in there for cups of coffee perhaps he'd have more time to visit church members in their homes. We have to pay for him, after all.

It is a good point. It goes to the heart of Christian ministry. Our priests and ministers cannot do everything in the church. There must be priorities. Members of the congregation should contribute their time, their energies and their talents to the work of the church. Even if they do so regularly and generously, it is still not possible for churches to do all the things that are desirable. Many churches are finding difficulty in sustaining the number of paid priests, ministers or workers that was accepted as normal even a generation ago. Many church members find it increasingly difficult to commit time to voluntary Christian service. Choices need to be made. Why should work in schools figure importantly in the priorities of churches? Should it take priority over the flower rota or sending relief to disaster areas?

The Church of England has moved steadily towards a policy of greater engagement with schools in recent years. In November 1998, the General Synod passed the following motion:

> That this Synod, believing that Church Schools stand at the centre of the Church's mission to the nation:
> (a) strongly urge:
> (i)   Diocesan Synods, in the light of the School Standards and framework Act, to review the resources available to Diocesan Boards of Education to enable them to be involved in all aspects of statutory education;

    (ii)   each PCC to discuss how it can serve all schools in the parish;

    (iii)   each PCC to commit itself to the greatest possible active support for Church schools in its area;

    (iv)   each Deanery Synod to consider how it can assist parishes in providing active support for Church schools which serve several parishes within its area;

(b) welcome the opportunities for Church schools to move to the voluntary aided category and encourages dioceses to support governors in so doing, where appropriate; and

(c) invite the Archbishops' Council to review the achievements of Church schools and to make proposals for the future development of Church Schools and Church colleges of further and higher education.

In November 2001 the Synod adopted the recommendations of Lord Dearing's Committee, which were published in *The Way ahead*, by passing the following resolution:

That this Synod ask

(a) the whole Church to build up the relationships described in the report, especially to ensure that Church schools are distinctively Christian institutions, rooted in the life of the parishes whilst being open to the diverse communities they serve;

(b) the dioceses actively to explore the opportunities for new Church schools, bearing in mind the Church of England's historic mission to serve the whole nation and its special care for areas of social disadvantage and the desirability for such schools to be ecumenically based;

(c) the whole Church at every level to promote the vocation to teach, and in partnership with the Church colleges of Higher Education to explore ways of supporting the professional and spiritual development of Christian teachers;

(d) the Archbishops' Council to require each of its Boards, Councils and Committees to discuss the implications of the report for their respective areas of responsibility and to draw up appropriate action plans to implement its recommendations;

(e) the Archbishops' Council to monitor progress on the implementation of the report's recommendations and to report back to the Synod in due course; and that this monitoring of progress pay particular attention (i) to the enhancement of a distinctively Christian ethos and approach in Church colleges of Higher Education; and (ii) to the appointment of committed Christian staff in these Colleges where these may be made on the basis of merit for the posts.

Locally there are many possible answers to the questions about the church's involvement with schools raised above. In order to stimulate thought and discussion a number of possible answers are offered in the following pages. These answers are described in terms of the approaches adopted by some churches or church members to the church's relationships with schools. In many churches individual church members will adopt one or more of these viewpoints and sometimes a view different from any described here. In areas where there is more than one church, the churches may differ in their styles and policies in relation to the schools in that location. The views selected and described here are designed to stimulate thought and discussion. They are not intended to be an exhaustive list.

Why should churches serve schools?

The Mallory or 'because they are there'

Mallory was a famous mountaineer before the Second World War. When he was asked why he climbed mountains, he replied, 'because they are there.' For many this may be the level at which the response to the question posed above is answered. Will it suffice as a response for church people who are looking ever more carefully at how time is used by priests, ministers and lay members of the church? Therefore, churches are forced to review their priorities. For some church people the response to a review will be that the existence of schools in the area around the church presents so many opportunities for service in the name of Christ that this alone is sufficient reason to justify the time spent. Others may need more convincing when they can identify many other conflicting claims on time and energy.

The Anglican or 'the cure of souls'

When Anglican priests are inducted into a new parish they are told that they are given 'the cure of souls' in the parish. This is to make it clear that they have a responsibility for everyone in the parish, not just those who attend church. This commitment to the parish as a whole is, at the same time, the strength and weakness of so many Anglican churches. It is a strength when it leads to selfless service to the community in the name of Christ, or when as a result it provides contact points for those who are searching, but have yet to find faith. It is weak when membership must be defined to justify requests for support from outside bodies or to prove that the rumour of the death of the church is exaggerated.

In relation to schools the 'Anglican' response argues that, if the parish priest is responsible for everyone in the parish, he or she must be concerned with the schools within that parish. It does not matter whether there are any church members in the school; that is not the point. The school is in the parish, which is all that is necessary to justify the time spent by the priest or other members of the church in its service. The unconvinced will say, 'So are the factory, the shopping centre and the sewage farm. Why should schools be high on the list?'

The Domestic or 'concern for "our" children'

The 'domestic' response focuses attention on the members of the church community, children or adult, who are also involved in the school. 'Our' children are being taught in these schools. 'Our' people are working in them. The church wishes to maintain contact and to become involved because of their care for their members. Such a proper concern to understand, to support and to share mutual commitments to children and adults may sometimes be misinterpreted by schools. Taken to extremes schools may respond as if they interpret such approaches as coming from a pressure group. Church members need to ensure that their approach is:

> I would like to talk to you because we share a mutual concern and commitment to these children.

and does not stress the negative aspects of the church's mission to education, for example:

> I want to talk to you because you are teaching our children and we want to know what you are doing.

or even

> I want to let you know that the congregation does not believe that you should be teaching our children . . .

(The reader is left to use their own experience to fill in the dots.)

Churches adopting the 'domestic' approach are showing the strength of their community and its care for its individual members. They are also providing practical evidence to local schools of the strength of Christian commitment in the area. These are clearly among the merits of such an approach. Those who wish to be critical of the 'domestic' response suggest that it could present the church as inward-looking, concerned principally with its own affairs and they would ask how this is reconciled with the call to evangelism.

The Mutual Interest

> We are both groups of concerned people trying to serve this community. We should work together for mutual support and encouragement.

This is much heard in areas where both churches and schools are under pressure perhaps because the values of both seem to be alien to those of the majority of the community in which they are placed. Taken to extremes the 'mutual interest' approach could be a sign that both school and church have become alienated from their local community. There are, however, many genuine areas of potential mutual interest and concern. Both churches and schools may share a love of children, a commitment to support parents or an anxiety about the social conditions in the area that they serve. The 'mutual interest' approach may develop very good relationships between the staff of the school and the staff of the church. Work that flows from this can be well founded and of more use to the community than either church or school can achieve on its own. It does, however, have the shortcoming that it identifies church people and teachers as outside the local community. As a response it can sometimes feel defensive.

The Traditional or 'we created this system anyway'

The churches took most of the early initiatives to create a system of schooling in this country that provides education for all. They did this by founding a large number of Church schools during the first 70 years of the nineteenth century. They have not surrendered the task to the State as they have done with so many other welfare and community tasks. There are a number of churches that are still committed to being part of the education system in this country, not least by maintaining schools within it. The Anglican Church has over 5,000 schools in the maintained system; the Roman Catholic Church over 2,500. While the appeal to historic and continuing involvement is an important justification for churches to work in schools, there will be many who wish to know where this is leading and what the churches' present and future vision is for their involvement in schools.

In different areas, or at different stages of the education system, the particular approach of Church schools may vary. Sometimes the governing body of a Church school will make it clear that the first commitment of the school is to provide a Christian education for the children of parents who are members of the denomination that founded the school. In other cases the governing body will state that its first priority is for the school to be of service to the neighbourhood by offering education to the children of all parents living in the area. This service is offered in the name of Christ, and within a school that is endeavouring to be a Christian community. Most Church schools, in practice, combine elements of both these concepts.

Both the Anglican and Roman Catholic Churches have sought to make their vision clear for their own schools, for example through the publication of *The Way ahead*. However, many members of these Churches, at local level, have yet to understand fully the reasons behind their denominations' continuing commitment to Church schools. (For more on Church schools see Part 2.)

The Consumer or 'we are as much clients of the system as any employer'

All churches are dependent on schools for the skills, knowledge and understanding that they teach. Christianity is a literate faith, in that it has a book, the Bible, as one of its foundations. Most Christians use the Bible in public worship as well as private study and devotion. Churches assume that most of their members can read with intelligence and discrimination. These skills are usually acquired in schools. In addition, the Churches need well-educated men and women to be its priests, ministers and leaders. Historically the Churches have provided their own schools and universities to fill this need. To some extent they continue to do so but in many places the State has taken over the provision. For most church members these are sufficient reasons for churches to maintain an interest in and commitment to schooling. Others point out that this view puts the churches alongside other interested consumers such as industry, commerce or the arts whose involvement in schools is less committed if sometimes better focused than that of the churches. Do the churches wish to find themselves classified as just another consumer group within education?

The Biblical or 'working with schools is part of our biblical ministry'

Two Gospel passages are often quoted when work with children and young people is discussed in church contexts. The first describes the incident in which parents are bringing their children to Jesus and the disciples are preventing them. Jesus rebukes his disciples and welcomes the children.

> Let the little children come to me, and do not stop them; for it is
> to such as these that the kingdom of heaven belongs.

> Matthew 19.14

From this incident it is clear that Christ welcomes children into the kingdom. If they are part of the kingdom then the Church should be seeking to serve them and witness to them wherever they are. For many this ministry will be achieved, in part at least, through work in schools.

The second passage is Jesus' three-fold challenge to Peter after the resurrection.

> When they had finished breakfast, Jesus said to Simon Peter, 'Simon son of John, do you love me more than these?' He said to him, 'Yes, Lord; you know that I love you.' Jesus said to him, 'Feed my lambs.' A second time he said to him, 'Simon son of John, do you love me?' He said to him, 'Yes, Lord; you know that I love you.' Jesus said to him, 'Tend my sheep.'

> John 21.15-16

Biblical scholars may point out that there is little difference in the Greek between the phrase 'feed my lambs' and the phrase 'tend my sheep' – both apparently intended to indicate that Peter was being given a pastoral charge for the people of God. Those who have a strong commitment to children, however, seek to make more of the difference. They point out that it was one of the leading apostles who was given the charge to 'feed my lambs'. They argue from this that today's Church leaders locally and nationally should follow Peter and accept their responsibility to give time and attention to work among children and young people.

As schools become more demanding of pupils' time and commitments, it is not surprising that many Church leaders are seeking to work with and in schools in their commitment to this aspect of their ministry.

The Industrial or 'education is a major employer and we should offer chaplaincy in the work place'

Education is a major industry. Over eight million people work in the education industry. Not all of these are paid, of course. There are the teachers and support staff. There are the governors, administrators, advisers and inspectors. The largest number of people working in the education industry are, however, the children and students themselves.

> What do you mean attending school is work? They only seem to play these days and anyway some of them like school so it cannot be hard work.

Ask any student working for GCSE or watch a group of young children wrestling with a problem and you will discover how hard the work can be. Enjoying what they are doing and working hard are not incompatible.

Education is indeed a major industry, carried out in small or large units in every community in the country.

The Churches provide a service of specialist chaplains for hospitals, the services and manufacturing, distribution and marketing industries. Within this model work undertaken by churches in schools is another form of industrial chaplaincy. There are already some people who are identified as chaplains to schools, particularly independent schools, to Further Education Colleges and to Universities. They could find their work more valued by the Church if this model were to be more widely adopted. Some church members will argue, however, that this model is dangerous because children and young people are not doing 'paid' work at school and that the industrial chaplaincy model may tend to emphasise the relationship and care that the churches should have with the staff of the schools rather than the pupils. Even if this is a weakness of the approach the 'industrial' does serve to emphasize the scale and importance of the challenge.

The 'Open all Hours' or 'we have a wonderful building and schools are welcome to visit us'

This approach has its roots in the importance to the community and the quality of the church buildings. In churches adopting this approach the building is an important meeting place – the focus of the local Christian community. Part of the mission strategy of such churches is to encourage people to come. Therefore, being open and accessible is a key part of their approach. At one extreme the great cathedrals with their visitor centres, bookshops and tea rooms are part of this tradition but so are the humble churches that strive to stay open all day despite the risks of theft and vandalism. Such churches will wish to create opportunities for schools to visit them. They will wish every local child to feel at ease and familiar with their building and will see encouraging school visits as an important part of this strategy.

Churches working in this way will be familiar with what is discussed in later sections of this book about preparing for school visits (see Chapter 8). They will also be ready with their answer to the critics who suggest that this approach places the church with the local museum and concert hall as places to visit and use that have no other important functions. In towns where redundant churches have been converted to such community uses the criticism will have an added dimension. How do churches that have a well-developed ministry to visitors

13

ensure that the prime purpose of the building as a place of worship is known and valued by all?

The Shrine or 'we have a wonderful building that is so holy that schools may visit us on certain conditions'

For some churches their building, or part of it, is such a 'holy' place that they feel uncomfortable and concerned about visitors, especially children, who may not know the rules, coming in and disturbing the character and atmosphere. They will put much effort into preparing their church to receive visitors and helping visitors to prepare themselves for their visits. Their members, who receive the visitors, will also be there to ensure that such visitors do not offend the rules and tradition. In many such churches there will be occasions during the year when the story of the 'shrine' or the place or things with which it is associated are celebrated. These occasions or records of them may provide a special opportunity to communicate some of the most important aspects of the faith.

The commitment of such churches to careful preparation and the maintenance of a worshipful atmosphere may make visits by children and young people a particularly important part of their spiritual development. Without such a commitment to help with preparation for a visit the 'shrine' approach can amount to putting padlock on the gate and erecting large signs saying 'no entry – members only'.

The Evangelical or 'we must preach the Good News in schools'

Many churches will be quick to recognize and own this approach. The Churches must present Christ to this generation of children in order to win them to the faith. This is a clear task of all the Christian churches.

> But by the open statement of the truth we commend ourselves
> to the conscience of everyone in the sight of God.
> For we do not proclaim ourselves; we proclaim Christ Jesus as
> Lord and ourselves as your slaves for Jesus' sake.
>
> 2 Corinthians 4.2-5

Is it however the best motivation for the churches' relationship with schools? Schools are places where meaning is explored and truth pursued in a safe environment, or at least they should be. Unless it is a Church school, work in the classroom about Christianity will be designed to enable pupils to understand what Christians believe and what it might mean to be a Christian. In many Church schools this will still be a strong theme. Some church schools, however, may also be able to make the assumption that their pupils are being brought up within Christian homes and thus present some aspects of their teaching about Christianity as learning about a shared faith.

There may be times when a church's commitment to evangelism and a school's concern for education about religion come into conflict. An example of this could arise when pupils need opportunities to explore with Christians what it means to them to be Christian. To be invited to attend a school to help students with this exploration is a privilege. To seek to use that invitation to challenge the pupils to make their own decision for Christ is to abuse the hospitality. Such challenges should be presented, but outside the school context and in places to which the children or young people have come voluntarily and perhaps even knowing that such a challenge will be made.

Some churches are so committed to the 'evangelical' approach that their representatives would feel unable to talk about their faith without presenting an explicit challenge to their hearers. Such churches should be open about this in their contacts with schools and only accept invitations to speak in contexts where the presentation of a challenge is appropriate. Some may feel that this limits what they, as churches or individuals, can do in schools, and may wish to put more energy into serving children and young people outside the school context. This should not prevent them from being involved in developing good relationships with their local schools or showing support for them.

The Witness or 'we want schools to see Christ in us'

This model draws on the tradition of selfless service, which has been part of the Christian commitment throughout the centuries.

> For I was hungry and you gave me food, I was thirsty and you
> gave me something to drink, I was a stranger you welcomed me,
> I was naked and you gave me clothing, I was sick and you took
> care of me, I was in prison and you visited me.

> Matthew 25.35-6

In serving others, Christians serve Christ. So in serving the schools and the children and adults in them, church members are offering service to their Lord.

In making their motives for this service clear they can make the claims of the gospel attractive. This may lead some to visit our churches or meetings in order to find out more. In visiting schools to explain or make clear what it means to them to be Christians they are also witnessing to the difference that their faith has made. In all of this they provide evidence that can lead others to further exploration.

This commitment is an honourable and continuing tradition within the churches. It is one that could have been easily undervalued in a Decade of Evangelism, which some Christians falsely believed was only about the evangelical approach outlined above. Many Christians who are teaching or working in other capacities in schools as part of their vocation would identify with this commitment to selfless service.

Critics of the approach would question whether the faith is ever made explicit within it. Churches or Christians who identify with this approach should be able to show how a recipient of their service would be able to identify that their motivation is their faith.

The Provider or 'this church has its own Church school for which it continues to provide financial support'

In provider churches the local congregation has a long-standing commitment to a voluntary aided school. Most of these churches will be Anglican or Roman Catholic. In voluntary aided schools 10 per cent of all the costs of improvements to the buildings must be borne by the governing body.[3] The provider church nominates a proportion of the governors and helps the governing body with its costs.

The parish priest will almost certainly be a member of the governing body and will give a significant proportion of each week to work in the school.

Provider churches benefit from having their own school. Research shows that they are likely to have more young people and adults involved in their activities than other churches that are not providers (Francis and Lankshear, 1993).

For most provider churches, the school is an important part of their service to the local community. In a few, sadly, where vision has been lost, their schools may be regarded as a drain on church resources. It seems obvious, but it is important to point out, that priests or ministers appointed to provider churches should be enthusiastic about the potential role of the school in the parish.

The Supporter or 'this church has its own church school but we don't put money into it any more'

Supporter churches have a voluntary controlled, foundation or an independent school with whom they are associated. Unlike provider churches they no longer have to make a financial contribution to the school but they may, through members on the governing body or the trust, have a significant stake in its management. Supporter churches are most likely to be Anglican or Methodist. The priest or minister responsible for the church will be on the governing body, will be active in the school and will probably undertake a regular commitment within the school's programme of worship.

Supporter churches are aware that much effective work is possible with their school if relationships are good and they will be committed to maintaining such relationships. Where such good relationships have been maintained over the years, supporter churches may be expected to benefit directly from their involvement in the school. Research results are less certain in this area because the issues are complex and so often affected by local circumstances (Francis, 1987a).

Some churches may have developed such good relationships with community schools they will recognize their work in this description.

The Young Family or 'we are very concerned about our ministry to children and their families'

These are churches where the majority of the worshippers are under 40, where worship takes account of the presence of children and where it is not uncommon to be welcoming recently born members to the family of the church.

In such congregations, local schools will naturally be one of the regular topics of conversation and, presumably, of prayer. The progress of church children through the schools will be known in general terms. Such churches are well placed to develop good relationships with local schools and also may be able to undertake activities designed to support Christian parents. They have particular experience of worship with children, which could be put at the service of local schools.

The most natural starting point could be the shared responsibility for children between church and school but the danger will always be that this becomes a concern for 'our' children which appears to exclude children not in the congregation.

The Older Generation or 'we don't have any children in our church. Is there any point in our contacting schools?'

Churches where the majority of the congregation is over 50, many having grandchildren, may have some hesitation about their involvement with schools. There are likely to be many members who fear that the presence of children and young people in church will disrupt the quiet, contemplative, worshipful atmosphere which they value.

Churches of this type, however, contain much wisdom and experience that could help schools. They may have members with time and energy that could be made available to schools in their area.

Conclusion

All these models are sustainable. All have their drawbacks. Christian churches and groups at work in the same area may be identifying with different models. Indeed many of the models may be held within the same congregation. Those models that churches feel closest to will, in part, determine the types of contact with schools into which churches commit time and energy. For example, a church adopting the evangelical model may wish to lead acts of worship in school, while one identifying with the witness model may free a member to serve on the governing body. Where churches in a locality differ about the models they wish to use and fail to discuss their different perceptions with one another, it is hardly surprising if they seek different types of relationships with local schools. Where this happens schools will receive very mixed messages with which they are unlikely to be able to cope. Churches and individual Christians need to be clearer about the models they are using and discuss these with each other in order to improve their relationships with local schools.

The range of Christian denominations that may be present or represented in an area further compounds these potential mixed messages from churches.

The majority of Christian churches are members of the Council of Churches in Britain and Ireland (CCBI) (see Appendix 1). In addition to the CCBI there are ecumenical organizations for England, Wales, Scotland and Ireland. At the local level there are many ecumenical groups often called 'Churches Together in . . .' or 'The . . . Council of Churches'.

Among each denomination there will be churches that are setting out to be the Christian church for a defined geographical area. While this is the Anglican and the Roman Catholic tradition, many other churches identify with it, not least where there is a shared or inter-denominational church. Other churches in all denominations will be serving a community of members drawn to that church because they value the fellowship, the community care, the style and tradition of worship or the doctrine for which that church is well known. Such eclectic congregations may have a lower commitment to the schools serving the community surrounding the church, but may relate more easily to schools or colleges that also draw from a wide area. For some eclectic congregations their most important contribution to work with local schools will be to support other churches or individuals to do it or to welcome visits from schools whose pupils need to experience the particular tradition of that church as part of their studies in religious education.

Part 2

Keeping up with the changes in education

3   *Understanding the task and the curriculum*

> In all circumstances, we would recommend that Church schools must be distinctively places where the Christian faith is alive and practised. Church schools will seek to offer excellence in education, and in so doing they will above all be concerned to develop the whole human being through the practice of the Christian faith.
>
> *The Way ahead* para 4.60

(Author's note: to be able to achieve 'excellence in education' in Church schools all those involved in contact with schools on behalf of the church must be aware of how 'excellence in education' is currently understood.)

You know how it is in schools. You can't mention God or Christ. You are not allowed to do anything that suggests worship. We had to move our congregation out of the school and convert a barn in which to worship.

The comment recorded above was made to the author with all the sadness of a gentle Christian soul caught up in a conflict over the appropriate use of a school building. It will find much understanding among church members who share some of these perceptions. It will be regarded as unbelievable by those who know schools. They will be puzzled as to how anyone in this country could so misunderstand what is being attempted in schools. This chapter is offered to help church people understand more about what is really happening.

Understanding the task

Imagine three people sitting at neighbouring tables in a restaurant. On the first table is Amy, who speaks five languages and works as an interpreter for the European Union. She is reading a book on fell walking. At the next table is Bertha who is involved in the development of the next generation of computers. While she eats her meal she is listening to a recording of Verdi's *Requiem* on her personal stereo. At the last table is Christine who works as a receptionist for the local doctor. While she is eating she is beginning to plan the design of her next embroidery project.

For each of these people schools will have provided an important part of the formal education that has equipped them to do their job and to follow their leisure interests. Schools have done the same for the waiter, the cook and all the others involved in the preparation of their meal. Schools are required to provide an education for everyone that will prepare them for 'the opportunities, responsibilities and experiences of adult life' (Education Act, 1996).

It is easy to forget the range of interests and abilities with which a school has to deal. In a class of 29 five-year-olds it may be difficult to discern which child will grow up to be a computer wizard, an artist, a footballer or a waitress – probably none of them. The education that is offered to all the children in the class must take account of and be appropriate for these and many other possibilities.

In the same class of five-year-old children:

- some of the children will come from homes where both parents are committed readers and books line the walls, while others will have seen adults in their home rarely reading anything but a newspaper or a TV listings magazine.

- most of the children will have been to nursery school or playgroup every day for the past two years, while a few will have remained in their home environment or with a child-minder until entering school;

- eight of the children are likely to have some contact with a Christian church and probably three or four with another faith, while the majority will have little or no contact with any community of believers.

No judgements should be implied from the above statements about what constitutes a better or worse situation. Given this range of experience, how do schools approach their task?

Understanding the curriculum

All schools in the maintained system (that is schools within the state sector) including Church schools in England and Wales, must use what the law calls the basic curriculum as the foundation for their teaching programme. The basic curriculum consists of religious education with the subjects of the national curriculum. The national curriculum subjects are English, mathematics, science, technology, history, geography, art, music, a foreign language (in secondary schools only), physical education and, in Wales, Welsh. The outline and basic content for each of the national curriculum subjects is developed in England by the Qualifications and Curriculum Authority (QCA) and approved by the Secretary of State. The QCA also arranges for the assessment of the progress of all school children at 7, 11 and 14 through a programme of testing, at 16 through GCSE and at 18 through A and AS levels, NVQs and other approved examinations. In Wales the Qualification, Curriculum and Assessment Authority for Wales (ACCAC) undertakes this work and approval is given through the National Assembly. Individual schools must work within this framework in the production of detailed programmes of work. In addition, every school is inspected every six years against a framework published by The Office for Standards in Education (OFSTED) and related to the national curriculum. There are equivalent arrangements in Wales for the assessment of pupils' progress and the inspection of schools. These are developed by Estyn, the Office of Her Majesty's Chief Inspector of Schools in Wales.

This pattern of national support for the curriculum created by legislation passed since 1988 still allows freedom for individual schools to choose methodologies and approaches that suit their own areas and the needs of the children living within them. In this context the unique position of religious education is important. Alone of the subjects that schools must teach by law, this subject has a locally agreed syllabus. These syllabuses are created by a conference that represents local interest groups including the Christian Churches. They may use national resources or work from other local authorities as a resource for their work. For most schools the Local Education Authority (LEA) is responsible for these locally but for voluntary aided schools, with a religious character, they are often determined by the relevant diocese or faith organization. Christian churches are required to be involved in the process of determining and supporting the LEA syllabuses for religious education through membership of local Standing Advisory Councils for Religious Education (SACREs) which are required by the Education Act 1996.

The spiritual, moral, social and cultural development of pupils

Since the passage of the Education Reform Act 1988 schools have been required to provide a curriculum that promotes:

> the spiritual, moral, cultural, mental and physical development of pupils at school and of society.

This is achieved in schools by planning a contribution from the programme of teaching, the 'hidden curriculum' and school worship. The Education (Schools) Act 1992 first provided for the inspection of these aspects of a school's task.

While it is usually assumed that schools understand about the mental and physical development of pupils, there exists no universally accepted definition of the words spiritual, moral, social and cultural in this context. Therefore it was a part of the curriculum that caused many schools and school inspectors considerable difficulty. Much work has been done to support schools in these areas, not least by some of the churches. There is now much greater understanding and experience in the field but policies for each of the four concepts, requiring a contribution from so many areas of a school's life, can be extremely difficult to coordinate.

Spiritual development

Christian churches will have their own understandings of what is meant by spiritual development. Such understandings will vary between churches in the emphasis they give to private prayer, public worship, service and self-discipline among other aspects of the Christian life. What is a community school with pupils from a number of different faiths to understand by spiritual development when each faith will have its own range of understandings? What does spiritual development mean to those who have no faith? Many schools will adopt a working definition that identifies the spiritual with the emotions and particularly with individuals' responses to the high and low points of human experience. Schools will seek to ensure that there are opportunities for pupils to reflect on their experience at school as part of the process of spiritual education. In addition, they will wish to teach pupils about the way in which different faiths respond to human experiences and feelings. Christian churches may be able to resource such work by providing people who can talk about their own spirituality, and by helping schools to plan work in this area. In some instances schools may use the facilities of a church to provide the atmosphere in which pupils can explore contemplation and reflection on their own lives and those of others. For those who wish to understand more about spiritual development in schools a good introduction is *Feeding Minds and Touching Hearts* by A. Brown and A. Seaman (2001).

Moral development

Much work has been done on the development of some aspects of moral understanding and behaviour among children and young adults. Less has been done to communicate this work to those outside the world of education. Young children learn first the way in which their family does things. When they come to school they may well find that how their family regards certain aspects of behaviour and how school regards them are quite different. This may not be because school and home are opposed but because the circumstances are different. In their early years at school, children will be encouraged to learn and abide by the school rules. This learning is usually reinforced by the presence of adults. The aim of such rules must be to help children to learn not only to obey but also to understand the benefits of obeying the rules. Only if this is achieved will children and young people come to accept them for their own, and therefore obey the rules even when there is no possibility of their being caught breaking them. Teachers working with children towards the later years of primary school will be familiar with this stage of moral learning.

> A dilemma for referees of football matches between primary schools is the advantage rule. In adult games it is accepted that if the rules have been broken but the side offended against wins some benefit from the situation, the referee does not have to take action. He or she can allow the game to proceed to play the 'advantage'. In primary school football, if the referee fails to stop the game for each breach of the rules, the game will come to a halt anyway, amidst cries of 'it's not fair!'

Later in their development, young people need to develop the understanding that many life situations are too complicated to be solved by the application of simple rules. Within the study of literature or religion there may be many occasions when the question 'Why did he do that?' leads to a moral debate. Here the difference between the rules that a person wishes to live by and the daily dilemmas of living become the fundamental stuff of moral education. Within this area the churches may be able to provide schools with individuals who are able to explain and discuss with young people how their personal faith provides the basis and the strength to resolve such dilemmas. It is unfortunate and at the same time natural that at the time when young people are wrestling with the acceptance for themselves of a standard or faith by which to live they are most liable to pressure from their peer group. Moral education is not as simple as some would have the public believe, nor does it automatically lead to socially acceptable behaviour – civil disobedience as a way of opposing unjust laws may be a morally appropriate action.

Social development
The first stages of the school's contribution to a child's social development take place in the first few weeks of a child's experience of school. In the family, children experience sharing the attention of one or two adults with perhaps one

or two other children. Sometimes children will have had the total attention of the adults in their lives. When children arrive at school or playgroup they have to learn to share the attention of the key adults with several other children. They have also to learn to cooperate with the other children in the group. From these early experiences grows an understanding of how to survive in and contribute to the school and, later, society in general. The experience of taking responsibility, raising money for charitable causes, caring for others and participating in making decisions are all aspects of the social development programme that schools provide. In some of these there may be opportunities for schools and their pupils to work in partnership with churches.

Cultural development

In their *Guidance on the Inspection of Nursery and Primary Schools* (HMSO, 1995) OFSTED give the following advice to inspectors.

> Cultural development is concerned both with participation in and appreciation of cultural traditions.
>
> The school's approach should be active. Inspectors need to look for evidence of how the school seeks to enrich its pupils' knowledge and experience of their own or other cultural traditions, through the curriculum and through visits, clubs and other activities. Aspects of the curriculum such as history, geography, art, music, dance, drama and literature can all make positive contributions, for example, through opportunities for pupils to:
>
> > visit museums and art galleries;
> >
> > work with artists, authors and performers;
> >
> > develop openness towards and value the music and dance of different cultures;
> >
> > appreciate the natural world through art and literature;
> >
> > recognise the contribution of many cultures to mathematics and to scientific and technological development.
>
> *Guidance on the Inspection of Nursery and Primary Schools*, Office of Standards in Education, 1995.

This guidance could be interpreted as taking a 'national' view of culture. It could lead some schools to think in terms of 'our' culture and 'other countries'' culture. There is a more complex view of this whole area, which could be included in an interpretation of this guidance. This view takes account of a range of different cultures existing and interacting within even quite small communities. For example, in music, the local culture could include the choral society, the jazz club, the folk group and Radio One, or in the performing arts, ballet, theatre, film or street performers. It may incorporate contributions from English, Scottish, Welsh, Irish, Caribbean, Indian or African cultures. One of the contributors to the culture of every area of the country will be the Christian Church not least through the music, art, literature it uses in its places of worship and its services.

Somehow the school must provide an introduction and opportunities to explore all of these cultures and many more. No one individual will appreciate or become involved in everything. All should be able to find and develop particular interests and should recognize and value the maintenance and development of traditions that are important in the life of the community or nation.

All four of these curriculum areas are important as they acknowledge that schooling is about more than just academic learning and preparation for the world of work. The problems for the schools lie in coordinating and resourcing what is taught and in finding the necessary time to achieve all that is desirable.

Concern and care for pupils

A further part of the way in which schools demonstrate their response to the local situation is their concern for their pupils. Many schools become deeply involved in work to help and support their pupils through difficult periods in their lives. They are likely to give considerable time and attention to pupils who

- are coming to terms with tragedy;

- experience problems relating to peers or adults;

- have difficulties in learning or have other special needs including those caused by outstanding ability in a subject or area of learning.

Class teachers or tutors, heads of year and headteachers are likely to be particularly involved in this work but all adults working in schools will have their contributions to make.

In many schools care and concern for their pupils will spill over into care and concern for their parents. It may be that, in some cases, the best way of helping the child is to help the parents. There is a tension here for schools. How much time should they spend helping and supporting parents, when their prime responsibility is to teach children? The challenge may be greatest in areas where there exists considerable social pressure and the other support agencies are, or seem to be, difficult for parents to contact. Schools are open every weekday during term time. There are teachers and other staff on duty from before nine o'clock until well after four, and there are often staff in the building before and after these hours and during holiday periods. Primary schools are usually within walking distance of children's homes. No wonder it seems easier for some parents to bring their troubles to the school than to other agencies whose points of contact may be less accessible.

4   *Understanding the hidden curriculum*

Church schools have the capacity to create an atmosphere in
which God can be discovered naturally and without apology. This
will include worship . . .

The Way ahead, para. 7.13

Worship

Every pupil in every school must attend an act of worship in school every day
unless the pupil's parents exercise their rights to withdraw their child under the
appropriate conscience clause. This means that even in the smallest school there
will be at least five acts of worship each week. In many schools, because worship
will sometimes be in key stage or year groups, there will be nearer ten. In some
large comprehensive schools, because worship is often conducted in tutor groups,
the number may reach over one hundred and fifty. In community schools the
majority of such services must be of a broadly Christian character. In Church
schools they will be within the tradition of the Church. This implies that the
headteachers or worship coordinators of most schools are responsible for
designing more acts of worship in a week than many priests or ministers,
and that without the benefit of a liturgical structure.

The daily act of worship may be an important opportunity for some children and
adults to worship God. For some others, perhaps, it will be their only opportunity
to discover what it might be like to worship. For the rest it will be a time when
they have to learn not to interrupt that which is important to others, even if they
feel unable to participate themselves. The act of worship may also be the time
when the school's values are made most explicit to children and to staff. In good
schools there will be careful planning of the worship programme and visitors
contributing to worship should be aware of how they are expected to fit into the
plans. They should also seek to establish some understanding of how many of the
school staff and pupils fall into each of the three categories described above, as
this should influence what they plan to do.

The hidden curriculum

Many men and some women have learnt that sport is so important that they
watch it for hours on television and read the sports pages of newspapers first.
Where and how was this attitude learned?

For many of them it will be the result of learning in school. This is not learning in the conventional sense of having someone set out to teach the concept. It is, rather, learning absorbed as a result of being part of an institution. We may begin to acquire the attitude that football is a more important issue than life and death by being part of institutions that convey that message by the amount of time, attention and importance they give to the two issues.

While statutory provisions determine the content of the subject curriculum, more is learnt in schools than that which is taught in lessons. This learning is sometimes referred to as 'the hidden curriculum'. It is part of the school's contribution to the passing on of national culture and attitudes. Some aspects of this are very good and important. We need to ensure that children are helped to grow up within a society whose better institutions and traditions they understand and value. For example, we all need to help pupils learn that courtesy and concern for others are not optional extras, but part of the basis on which living in an overcrowded island can become tolerable. Most people will regard some aspects of the 'hidden curriculum' as essential and positive. Their views of other aspects, such as the attitude to sport mentioned above, will differ. Some people may regard one or two aspects as negative: they may perceive the school as encouraging an attitude to male behaviour that suggests that 'big boys don't cry' and find this inappropriate for their own children.

Provision of alternatives

> When he grows up he will be a docker, just like his father and grandfather before him.

This has been an unlikely statement for almost a generation, but there are many equivalent statements that may still have some currency. If it were likely or possible for most children to follow their parents' footsteps then we would probably not need schooling at all. The whole development of school derives from the need to provide a level and range of education for children that can take them beyond their parents' circles of experience and knowledge.

Personally, I have often had cause to be thankful my children were not limited by my lack of knowledge of chemistry or geography. Within the schools that they attended there were teachers who had greater knowledge of and enthusiasm for these subjects than I have ever possessed. I am grateful that this knowledge and enthusiasm was made available to my children. This is a simple example to illustrate a profound point. If schools exist, in part, to provide alternatives for children and young people then care needs to be exercised over the rhetoric that suggests that 'parents know best'. There is a tension here. Parents should support their own children and their interests, but in partnership with schools not with battle lines drawn.

A further illustration may be useful to stress the importance of this point. Children entering school at the age of five in September 2002 will reach the earliest point at which they are currently allowed to leave in June 2013. Their working lives could last until 2062, assuming that retirement stays at the same age as now. Schools are now preparing children for adult experiences into the middle of this century and beyond. The work requires some considerable thought about what such experiences might be.

Only just over 30 years ago the electronic calculator was being demonstrated on the BBC's *Tomorrow's World* as a remarkable new device. The first model cost over £100. If that gives an indication of the pace of change that we have experienced in 25 years, for what changes are we preparing our children!

Teachers, parents, governors and all concerned with education need to be joined in a commitment to develop the education of our children for the second half of this century. The churches have an important part to play as supporters, contributors and partners in this complex process. The churches need to ensure that in seeking and accepting such involvement they have an understanding of what schools are required to attempt for their children.

Whenever a new priest or minister is to be appointed to a church the congregation should be asked to prepare a profile of the area in which their church is set. This is important in ensuring that the person appointed knows what work is expected or possible. Included in that profile should be details of local schools. For churches that regard engagement with the locality as important, these school details and the response of potential appointees to them will be crucial. Where work with schools is a key factor, care should be taken to ensure that potential appointees know this and by their attitude and experience show that they can fulfil this part of their expected ministry.

It is important that churches understand the organization of schools in their area and, as a result improve their contacts with them. Confusion and irritation can arise if incorrect or misleading terms are used.

> Don't they know that 'Playschool' was the name of a television programme?

Don't they realize that a nursery class and a playgroup are not the same thing?

Summary

This chapter has described some of the tasks that face a school today. These have included dealing with a range of abilities and experiences, curriculum issues, the spiritual, moral, social and cultural development of pupils, concern and care for pupils and their parents, school worship, the hidden curriculum, the provision of alternatives and anticipating the needs of pupils preparing for adult life in the next century. Care has been taken to avoid the use of jargon and to explain the terms used. In the resources and further information section there is a guide to different types of school and the meanings of some of the key words used in education (see Chapter 9). Leading or working in a school is a complex task requiring great energy and professionalism. Churches who are seeking to serve schools need to develop their understanding of all these issues.

Part 3

What can churches do to serve schools?

5   An important 'health warning'

This section of the book is designed to be positive and encouraging but damage can be done to relationships between churches and schools unless some issues are clearly understood. This warning notice needs to be read and understood by all church people so that they approach schools with sensitivity.

Church members who volunteer to help schools should understand that

1.   The headteacher is responsible for everything that happens in the classroom, in the school and to school parties out on visits.

2.   Church members who accept invitations to work in schools are working for the headteacher.

3.   Helpers need to be aware of the school's policies and ensure that while they are in the school they conform to them in order to ensure that what they do supports and reflects the ethos of the school.

4.   Helpers should not be offended if they are asked to complete the procedure to obtain formal police clearance of their suitability to work with young children. This is part of routine procedures to ensure that children are as safe from harm in schools as they are in their families or in churches.

If individual church members cannot accept this discipline work in or with schools should be left to others.

In the chapters that follow the phrase 'church ministerial team' is used to cover all those who are in contact with schools on behalf of their church. It is intended to cover the paid priest or minister, if there is one, as well as voluntary priests, ministers, elders, church leaders, leaders of church children's groups and any other member to whom the church has given its authority as a representative. It does not necessarily cover all church members who are parents at the school or who happen to enter the school building.

6   *The essentials*

Parishes and schools should pray regularly for each other.

Recommendation from *The Way ahead*

Good relationships between churches and schools are essential. From the church perspective a proper concern for the children in the area that they are serving, some of whom will be in contact with the church through Sunday worship or weekday activities, is part of the church's commitment to witness to Christ by service to the local community.

There will be some churches whose major involvement with the local community will be to present the challenge of the gospel through evangelism. Among their members will be those who preach Christ in the marketplace and on doorsteps. This is an important ministry conducted in circumstances where people are free to walk away or close the door. It builds on the experience and knowledge of Christians and the gospel story gained by those to whom it is addressed. Its place in schools is within meetings of voluntary societies or clubs. It is not appropriate in the classroom where pupils are required, unless parents make formal objection, to be present or in school collective worship unless undertaken with the full prior knowledge and agreement of the school staff. There may be times when members of such congregations are invited into classes to be asked why they present the gospel in the way that they do. Such occasions are an opportunity to explain 'What my faith means to me and how it affects my life'. They should not be exploited as opportunities to challenge pupils to make their own decision for Christ. Stories that circulate among teachers about abuses of hospitality of this type are among the reasons why Christians may find themselves viewed with suspicion by schools and may lead, in extreme cases, to access to a particular school being denied to all representatives of the Christian churches.

Within the range of Christian churches that exist in this country there are perhaps five broad groupings with which every child should have had some contact during their programme of learning about Christianity. These are the Anglicans, the Roman Catholics, the Free Churches, the Orthodox and the Pentecostal. Within these groupings there are important differences of emphasis and tradition and, more significantly, much that is held in common. In any area particular denominations or traditions within each grouping may be able to offer particular strengths. By coming to know something about churches within each grouping children and young people will be helped to:

- identify the range of liturgical and free worship used by Christians week by week;

- hear the range of music used by Christians in worship;

- understand the importance to Christians of the Bible;

- gain knowledge of the different ways in which Christians express their sense of community with each other;

- appreciate Christianity as a world faith through the variety of links which these groups have worldwide;

- identify the different ways in which Christians express their spirituality.

It may be helpful to schools if the churches in a particular area from these different traditions are seen to be working together in their contact with schools and to be mutually supportive in this work.

From a school perspective, given that at least a quarter of children are in some form of contact with a Christian church (Francis and Lankshear, 1988), it will be important for schools to have some knowledge of the experience that children are gaining through their church and its organizations. This is of particular importance in schools where the children give their teachers the impression that 'none of them go to church'. Of course there will be a few schools where no children are in contact with a Christian church, but these are very few compared with the number of schools who claim that situation. Schools will not know whether they really have no children who go to church unless they are in regular good contact with the churches serving their area.

Perhaps the most important first step in establishing good relations between church and school is to ensure that the staff of the school come to know the church's ministerial team as people. This implies that there should be opportunities when members of the ministerial team can talk with the staff informally, perhaps about mutual interests, which will naturally include the children and parents that they both seek to serve and the circumstances in which they are trying to work. Churches and schools have a range of tasks and priorities some of which they share and some of which are complementary, therefore, there exist a number of reasons for dialogue. It is certainly helpful if schools come to understand the work that the churches are seeking to do and likewise the churches understand the schools.

Good relationships between ministerial teams and school staff are important but they are not an end in themselves; they are the gateway through which much mutually helpful work can develop once a sound basis has been created.

In the chapters that follow this, some suggestions will be made for areas of service that churches could offer to schools. No single church could be doing everything. There are limits to time and energy. These chapters will represent more than the minimum that could be expected of any church. This minimum, however, does exist. There are a number of things that all churches should be offering in service to their local school or schools. This chapter will suggest five distinct activities that every church could and should offer, within an ecumenical framework where possible.

1   Prayer

In churches where there is a prayer leaflet, each local school could appear on it, preferably with the names of key staff. This would help develop a powerhouse of private and individual prayer in support of the schools. They should also be remembered in public prayer regularly, not just at the beginning of the school year. A better pattern would be at the beginning and end of each term, on Education Sunday, at examination time in the summer and on the occasion of known special events in school. This would create a pattern of public prayer that would see schools mentioned about once a month through the year, with a special focus in the service on Education Sunday. Chapter 15 contains a number of prayers drawn from various sources, which may be useful in this context. Chapter 16 contains a table showing a selection of the significant points in the Christian year and the school's year, which is designed to help churches plan their pattern of prayer for schools and teachers.

2   Befriending

There should be at least one person, probably a member of the church ministerial team, who knows each local school and is known by it as a representative of the church, and a link between school and church. In most churches the identity of this person will be obvious and the choice natural, but some care is needed to ensure that the person is able to create the positive atmosphere within which further links could be developed.

3   Positive support

Local churches should be supportive in their attitudes in order to help schools in achieving their aim. Staff and governors should know that their work is valued. Teachers, particularly Christian teachers, should be encouraged and their achievements celebrated. Many churches try to do these things but then allow the impact to be damaged by failing to challenge the comment of those who are so shrivelled in spirit that they can only repeat the unthinking criticism peddled by the destructive in our society. Comments like

> In my day we were taught to read properly,

heard when a child stumbles over a word when reading a passage in church, or

> Of course the exams are easier now,

in response to hearing the achievements of the church's young people are wrong and deeply damaging – they must be challenged. Left lying they

● drive youngsters from the church;

● hurt teachers who have laboured with pupils to produce the results;

● damage the church's good relationship with schools.

Said by individuals in church the damage may be limited, written by a member of the church's ministerial team in the local press, such remarks can reduce relations between the churches and local schools to a frosty politeness at best.

4   Welcome ministries

Every church should consider how it welcomes visitors and the purpose for which they might come. Some of the preparation for welcoming could have the effect of making the church more accessible and welcoming to non-school visitors as well. (see Chapter 8 for details.)

5   Free for ministry

Some church members may already be giving their time to work in schools or for schools locally as governors, SACRE members, volunteers or members of staff. If does not require much time or effort to ensure that such people know that they have their church's support for this work. It may take some restraint to ensure that busy people are not forced to choose between their ministry for schools and their ministry within the church. Someone else might organize the church social events in order to free the time of a fellow member of the congregation to maintain their work in schools.

A church that does not do these five things should consider seriously its attitude to schools. A church that is doing these five but no more is probably missing opportunities; that church should study the following chapters to explore what further work might be possible. A church that is doing more than these five things and is coordinating its work with other local churches may be able to sustain a claim to be serving its local schools.

Points for thought, discussion and action

List the schools in the area served by the church.

For each one list

- Who in our ministerial team is involved in promoting our relationships with this school?

- Who in other churches' ministerial teams is involved?

- Is the situation good or does it need more work?

7　*Commissioning for service*

> The Church should affirm Christian teachers through pastoral
> visits to schools . . . . And through inviting Christian teachers in
> Church and Community schools, including Special Schools to
> appropriate events.
>
> Dioceses should show the importance the Church attributes to the
> appointment of headteachers by a Service of commissioning of the
> kind that has been agreed in some dioceses.
>
> Recommendations from The Way ahead

The vocation to teach

As with any profession there is a body of knowledge and a range of skills that
must be acquired before teachers can be regarded as competent. However, the
satisfaction gained from competency in a complex profession is not the reason
why most teachers continue to attend their place of work each day. For many,
a main motivation is a commitment to the children they teach. For a significant
number their faith in Christ is also part of their motivation. For the Christian
teacher, teaching is part of discipleship and a response to Christ's command to
follow him. A survey conducted a few years ago on the background of teachers,
indicates that there was then a higher proportion of Christians in teaching than
could be expected from the number of Christians in the population as a whole
(Francis, 1987b).

Nothing involving the motivation of people to undertake a task is ever
straightforward. Visiting a school towards the end of a term and listening to
the conversation in the staff-room may create the impression that teachers are
tired, cynical and only too eager to escape from the profession. This human
response to a difficult environment should not blind church people to the real
level of commitment within the profession and the significant number of teachers
for whom teaching is still a vocation. Some teachers will have entered their
profession with this sense of vocation already developed. Others develop such
a vocation through the work that they do.

The churches need to find ways of developing, encouraging and affirming the
vocation to teach in the schools in their locality, not only among young people
but also among those who have maturity and experience of the world to offer,
alongside other gifts to the children that they will teach.

How do Christians become teachers?

Many churches have provided routes into teaching in school by encouraging those members who have a talent for working with children and young people. The first steps towards a commitment to teach in school have often been taken through experience of work in Sunday schools, children's or youth groups or uniformed organizations based in churches.

The question that often arises is 'how can we help these Christians find the most appropriate route for them into teaching?'. Teaching is largely a graduate profession and, therefore, most entrants will need to obtain a degree as part of their preparation for their vocation. This is important for two reasons: firstly it would be very odd if a teacher were to be encouraging a class to work hard at their education when the teacher was not committed to his or her own learning; secondly, teaching is not just a Christian vocation, it is also a profession. It is neither acceptable nor appropriate for those who are entering the profession as a result of a clear sense of vocation from God to be any less professional about their work than those who approach teaching as a career.

One of the obvious routes into the profession is through the courses offered by the Church Colleges of Higher Education. These colleges offer a range of degree courses and several different routes into teaching through degree courses that carry 'qualified teacher status' or through Postgraduate Certificates in Education, for those who already hold a first degree. Most of them also offer specialist courses in the work of Church schools and a wide range of opportunities to study aspects of theology. For those with the ability to teach but without the formal qualifications to begin studying for a degree, there are special 'access' arrangements. Some of the courses in theology can also provide a basis for building up credits. Dioceses may use some of these courses to supplement their programmes of adult Christian learning. The Church colleges are a good choice for many Christians coming into teaching because they offer a Christian context for study, with the chapel at the heart of college life, and also have an understanding of Christian vocation.

In choosing a college, it may be helpful to ask about the existence of:

- the Church College Certificate programmes in religious studies, Church schools studies and related themes;
- pathways to training that include experience of work in Anglican schools;

● for those who are committed to higher levels of study, the existence of the Master's degree programme in Church school education.

Another route into teaching can be through school-based training. There are a number of such schemes involving Church schools and at least two that are sponsored by dioceses (London and Hereford).

In order to assist members of parish ministerial teams in providing advice on these issues, a list of the Church colleges and of diocesan education offices is contained in the appendices (Appendices 2 and 4). Advice on routes into teaching can also be obtained from the Teacher Training Agency.

Nurturing teachers

It is one thing to ensure that vocations to teach are encouraged, it is quite another to seek to support those who are already exercising the Christian ministry of teaching. Work done in churches to encourage the vocation to teach of itself shows the value given to teaching as a ministry, and is part of the support of Christian teachers in the congregation. Nevertheless, most churches will wish to do more. They will want to reach out to teachers and others working in local schools in order to demonstrate to them that their commitment and work is valued by the churches. One regular opportunity is provided by Education Sunday, which is now celebrated by most of the major Churches in this country. This Sunday, the ninth Sunday before Easter, was chosen partly because the theme of the Eucharist in the Church of England's *Alternative Service Book 1980* (ASB), was 'Christ the Teacher'. Although the ASB is no longer authorized for use in Church of England churches, the theme has become so well established ecumenically that it seems unlikely that there will be serious moves to change the designated Sunday. If this Sunday is observed and teachers are regularly prayed for during services, perhaps particularly at the beginning and end of school terms, then the teachers in the congregation will know that there is a concern for them as a group. Christian teachers are individuals, however, and, like most Christians, will need the opportunities provided by such activities as house groups or meetings with Christian friends to share their story, and to discuss their concerns and worries. Failure to provide such opportunities and to remember the needs of teachers and schools in prayer is a signal that the church is not concerned with them in their vocation.

Unfortunately, failing to show care may not be the most unhelpful path that a church can follow in respect of the teachers and potential teachers within their congregation. In some places congregations are trapped into accepting an idea of the work of teachers and schools that is put about by those whose motives are destructive. Unthinking, insensitive, ill-informed or destructive criticism of education in general and the work of teachers in particular can have a devastating effect on both members of the congregation who are committed to teaching as an expression of their discipleship, and Christian teachers in local schools.

There will be some who will argue that this section overstates the case for the support of Christian teachers, but the issue is very important and therefore needs to be energetically argued. Teaching in schools and colleges is not just a matter of exercising certain skills and knowing more about a subject than the group that is being taught. Teaching has important links with the performing arts in so far as the best teachers are able to summon enthusiasm for their topic and convey this to their pupils. To do this they have to be prepared to make themselves open to their pupils and, therefore, take the risk of becoming vulnerable. The way in which teachers feel about themselves and the task in which they are engaged is vitally important to the quality of their teaching. The morale of teachers is crucial to the success of education. Churches have a duty to ensure that Christian teachers are encouraged and supported in their vocation for the good of the teachers themselves, for the quality of learning of the pupils and, therefore, for the values of the witness that they provide.

The above paragraphs have emphasized the importance of supporting the Christian vocation to teach. This should not be interpreted to mean that churches should only be interested in or value the work of Christian teachers. There are many good teachers who are totally committed to their work and the children they teach, who are not Christians. The local Christian church should demonstrate that their right to their own beliefs is respected and that they are valued as colleagues, co-workers for the children and friends.

How do Christians who are teachers become Christian teachers?

At first glance this may seem a strange question to ask, but it lies at the heart of a major challenge to the churches. It may be helpful also to ask the question the other way round. What prevents a Christian who is a teacher from becoming a Christian teacher?

The challenge here is for people who are living lives in which their faith is dissociated from their work. This is not uncommon. If churches share the vision of vocation developed by Rowan Williams, the Archbishop of Wales in *The Way ahead* (for full text see web site www.natsoc.org.uk) they will seek to find ways of helping church members develop their understanding of how their faith relates to their lives outside the church. Churches can achieve this by:

- preaching about the relationship between faith and daily life;
- teaching on these issues in study groups and home groups;
- ensuring that the worship includes an element that is outward-looking and reflects the life and work of the congregation;
- ensuring that the community life of the church engages with the local community;
- ensuring that the church offers opportunities for individuals to reflect on their faith and experience outside the church community.

Sadly, too many teachers experience criticism of their work personally and as a profession from the inspection process, from the media and sometimes from the churches. Within the world of education there is often criticism of the churches, some of which is ill-informed prejudice, but some of which is fed by the action of individuals speaking for or on behalf of the churches. Teachers have to find ways of coping with this negative element in their professional lives. Teachers who are also Christians have to deal with this on two fronts. Not surprisingly, this tends to encourage individuals to create barriers and defence mechanisms in order to be able to manage. In extreme cases this can lead to teachers separating their professional lives from their lives in the church community. They become, or remain, teachers who are also Christians. Churches need to work at this area by being supportive, by being very careful about how they express criticisms of what they perceive to be the short-comings of the education system and by being very sensitive to the pastoral needs of members of their congregations. Work undertaken in line with the suggestions in the previous paragraph should also help in this area.

Focused prayer

One of the most powerful ways of helping Christians who are teachers become Christian teachers is through prayer. Merely stating this truism is not sufficient. The statement needs to be broken up so that we are clear what it means and how churches should set about it.

1   Helping teachers pray about their work

It is important that churches pray for pupils and teachers in general. Teachers should be helped to develop their own prayer life in a way that focuses down on their own work, joys, challenges and worries. Some may find *Pocket Prayers for Teachers* (Lankshear, 2002) useful as a stimulus for this.

2   Listening to teachers and responding

Where teachers are part of groups within a local church, these groups should ensure that from time to time they pay particular attention to what the teachers wish to share and then offer that to God in prayer. Some teachers and some church members may find extemporary prayer difficult, but this should not excuse them from being explicit and focused in their prayer. Chapter 15 provides a selection of prayers from liturgical and other sources, which can be used or adapted for these purposes.

The aim of these activities is to support and extend the public, general prayers of the church for schools and for teachers with private specific petition, intercession and thanksgiving.

Time

Everything that has been written above implies that there is time available to do the things that are necessary within each congregation for individual Christians. There needs to be

- Time to talk together;
- Time to listen to each other;
- Time to pray;
- Time to listen to God;
- Time to grow in understanding of our faith;
- Time to grow in understanding of our discipleship.

This is not a task for public worship alone, although public worship is important. Nor is it a task for the minister or priest alone, although their roles can be vital. Every Christian is involved as far as the Spirit enables them. Every Christian has needs in this area and also something to give.

Helping Christian teachers grow in their faith and their profession

This section explores the ways in which the churches can support and should be supporting Christian teachers.

Encouraging spiritual growth

For all Christians, growth in the Spirit is the sign of life as a Christian disciple. There is no standing still. There is growth and development or there is decline and decay. This is also true professionally. There is growth and development as a teacher or there is stagnation. Therefore, spiritual growth for a Christian teacher will seek to combine growth in the faith with professional growth. One of the things that marks out the Christian teacher from the teacher who is also a Christian is the interaction between professional and spiritual growth.

For some Christian teachers this will best be supported by Christian teaching that is drawn out from their experience of the world of work. Home groups or small group meetings may be the setting for such discussions where Christians are encouraged to share issues, challenges, joys and opportunities from their work or home life that can be discussed and reflected in the light of the faith.

For others it will be the teaching of faith that comes first. There is a particular skill given to some Christian ministers that enables them to teach the gospel in a way that encourages listeners to reflect on its specific meaning in their own lives.

> Is it nothing to you, all you who pass by?

In contrast, closed teaching, which permits only one meaning, requires no response other than acceptance or rejection and is unlikely to create the interaction with professional growth that is desirable in the Christian teacher.

Among Christian teachers will be those who are already, or who are preparing for, exercising of Christian leadership, perhaps as a headteacher of a Church school. Such public Christian roles make great demands and call for considerable spiritual resources. In the main these will only be developed in the context of the Christian congregation with whom they worship.

Time and support

In the previous section the importance of time was discussed. It will be apparent that Christian teachers must also create, and be given time to develop and renew, their spiritual resources. They also need the support of their fellow Christians in their work. The fact that they are both skilled professionals and strong in the faith does not reduce their need for support or the effect of indifference or criticism on them.

Practical example

One of the practical ways in which churches can show the importance that they attach to the Christian vocation to teach is to provide opportunities for teachers to renew their commitment and to be commissioned into a new role. Many dioceses have provided commissioning services for new headteachers of Church schools. These have been an important occasion for the individuals and for their schools. In Chapter 14 there are two short services. The first is designed as an act of renewal of commitment and could be incorporated in an Education Sunday service or used during regular Sunday worship, perhaps at the beginning of the school year. The second is an act of commissioning for service. This has been developed out of commissioning services already in use in some dioceses and is suitable, not just for headteachers, but for any teacher taking up a new post.

The headteacher – a special case?

To be appointed as a headteacher, a teacher must have demonstrated ability and energy in a number of more junior posts in schools. They will have given considerable time to training and education beyond their initial degree or professional qualification. They are responsible for a wide range of activities in school, including many for which their initial professional education will have been an inadequate preparation. One of the unintended effects of much of the recent debate about education has been to lower their prestige and respect in the community while the legislation springing from the debate has increased their responsibilities. Churches must not be tempted to undervalue the importance of the role of the headteacher, nor should they make the common assumption that associates the size of the school or the age of its pupils with the prestige of the post. Some of the most demanding headships are in small primary schools.

Headteachers are often portrayed as the ones who inhibit the development of co-operation, in much the same way the priests or ministers are portrayed as the ones who hold back their churches. The similarity is, of course, that in both cases the responsibility for administration and organization depends on them at the day-to-day level. Schools and churches exist for different purposes, although they share some objectives. It is not surprising if, on occasions, the people who carry the responsibility have to say 'no'. This should be understood and accepted. Carrying the responsibility can be a lonely activity, particularly when the traditional support services are being eroded. Good relationships between the church ministerial team and the headteacher may not only facilitate much of the cooperation covered in this book but may also provide part of the support structure that all headteachers need in order to function effectively.

'Support' staff

In many schools there will be more staff who are not teachers than there are teachers. Many of these people will be active members of local churches, and will bring their own understanding of how their faith affects their life to their work. Often such staff work in posts that carry low status. Lunchtime supervisory staff, caretakers, cleaners, special needs assistants, nursery nurses and school secretaries do not figure in the top ten professions but they are a vital part of the school's work and all of them may have regular contact with children and, in some cases, parents. Some of them will contribute significantly to the caring work that the school undertakes. The care shown for worried parents by a school secretary can do much to help them express their concerns and receive the help or reassurance that they need. At times of sickness in a school the maintenance of a clean environment in general and clearing up after children who have been ill is most important. The responsibility for this rests with the caretaking and cleaning staff. There are some inner city primary schools where the school caretaker not only has to endeavour to keep the premises secure during the night but must also inspect the grounds each morning before the children arrive to ensure that material used and then discarded by drug addicts does not remain in places where children might touch it.

None of the work undertaken by the support staff in school is easy and all of it is responsible. The people undertaking such work need to know that what they are doing is valued by the churches and the local community. Those who are members of our congregations need to feel that the school in which they are working, and their own contribution to it, are supported and upheld in prayer by their church.

Earlier in this chapter the services of commissioning and recommitment were mentioned. There is every reason why they should be extended to include other staff in schools and school governors. The text of these two acts of dedication may be reproduced for use in churches or schools, without obtaining copyright clearance.

Points for thought, discussion and action

1. What action are we taking in our church to support the Christian vocation to teach or work in the service of schools?
2. Do we celebrate Education Sunday? If not, why not?
3. What are other churches in our area doing? Could we work together?
4. Think of all those in the congregation who are involved in education. What do their jobs involve? How can we support them better?

8 *Contributing to school activities*

Clergy who are seen to be at home and effective in a school,
and who are respected by teachers for their professionalism,
may well find that there is a welcome for them, and the
opportunity to make a valued contribution, in a goodly
number of community schools.

The Way ahead, para. 7.2

Worship

Much has happened in school worship in recent years that should be welcomed
by the Churches. Many schools have developed good policy documents and have
developed their approach to planning the programme of worship in the school.
This should change the way in which schools plan the visits of those they invite
to help lead worship and the way in which these visitors contribute. In the future,
schools will expect visitors to be able to contribute to the school's plans and to
lead worship within the style and pattern established in the school. Visitors who
insist on doing things their own way and who cannot adapt to the ways of the
school will probably find the number of invitations that they receive reducing.

Many schools will look for opportunities to invite members of local ministerial
teams to contribute to such programmes. However, the contribution could be in
the planning as well as in the delivery, and does not necessarily mean that they
should be asked to lead the whole of every act of worship for which they are
present. Most schools will wish to plan their programmes of worship with care,
and this provides a further opportunity for members of ministerial teams to make
a valuable contribution, not least in helping teachers identify the range of worship
ideas that are part of the Christian tradition, and that could be used within a
lively programme of school worship.

Not every member of a ministerial team will be good at leading school worship
with all age groups. Some may not feel comfortable with any school age children.
No one should feel compelled to take part if his or her talents do not lie in this
area. Any who do take part must accept that, as with work in the curriculum,
when they are in school to lead an act of worship, the headteacher carries the
ultimate responsibility for what they do and say. It is very important that they
understand that they must operate within the school policy on worship, and that
they should be aware of the way in which their contribution has to fit into the

overall programme of worship in the school. Much has been written about school worship (e.g. Barton, Brown and Brown, 1994 and Bailey, 1999,) and there is no point in repetition. However, the advent of the arrangements for inspection following the Education (Schools) Act 1992 has led to many schools reviewing their policies on worship, and the expertise available to them within the local community continues to be invaluable in the process.

Local churches may be able to provide this help, both through the practical experience and expertise of their ministerial team or by putting the school in touch with experts employed by the churches in this field.

Some schools may not be aware that many Churches have good quality published material that can help the school with its worship. The local churches should be able to bring such material to the school's attention by providing catalogues, arranging displays or lending sample copies. In many parts of the country, church organizations can provide training which, by helping people to explore the issues and helping them practise preparing and delivering acts of worship for schools, can build confidence and expertise. Local churches should be able to provide information to schools about what is available from their denomination. There is also useful material available on web sites such as www.natsoc.org.uk and www.churchschools.co.uk.

Some schools find it difficult to make proper use of help from local churches because of what they perceive as local church rivalries.

> I can't invite Mr Bloggs from the Baptist Church any more, despite the fact that he is brilliant with our children because, if I do, I will have to invite someone from each of the other denominations and one or two of them are hopeless.

This has been said by so many headteachers that it is time the churches did something about it. The local meeting of clergy or council of churches should be able to identify the gifts that Mr Bloggs has been given by the Spirit in this regard and authorize him to work for them all in taking acts of worship in local schools. If they cannot, what is this saying about the spirit of ecumenism that should exist between them?

School Eucharists

In some schools, usually Church schools, it will be right for there to be celebrations of the Eucharist. Members of church ministerial teams may have a special part to play in these. Some celebrations of the Eucharist may be part of the regular programme of collective worship in the school and, as such, there may be many children and some staff attending the service who are not confirmed or in full adult membership of a Christian Church. Some may not be Christians. Many parents, if they are invited to be present, may also not be able to receive communion. Special sensitivity is needed in planning such services. Creative use of the liturgy will be important, as will careful thought about such things as how the administration will be managed. Great care will be needed in such services to ensure that all those who are present are enabled to take part as fully as possible in the service.

In a number of schools, celebrations of the Eucharist will be voluntary and occur either before school, after school or during the lunch break. They are likely to be attended by committed Christians among the staff and pupils and are a focus for prayer about the school as a whole and an opportunity for Christians involved in the school to be strengthened and to encourage each other. Care needs to be taken to ensure that even where the numbers attending are small compared to the number of adults on the staff or the number of pupils in the school, the celebration is part of the life of the school and not separate from it. The prayer focus will be the whole of the school not the Christian minority. Church ministerial teams may well be able to contribute to these from their experience of celebrating Eucharists for small groups who know each other well.

The celebration of the Eucharist in school needs careful consideration, preparation and sensitivity even in a Church school. There will be many Church primary schools that do not have such a celebration. In community schools the complexity involved in having a Eucharist involving the whole school or a significant section of it will mean that it happens rarely. It is less uncommon to find community schools where there is an occasional opportunity to attend a celebration being held by an informal Christian group or club within the school.

Religious education

All religious education teaching in community and some voluntary schools should be rooted within a planned programme of work related to a Local Authority Agreed Syllabus. In voluntary aided schools that have a religious character, religious education must be conducted in accordance with the Trust Deed of the school. Usually this will be achieved by following the appropriate diocesan syllabus.

The Local Authority Agreed Syllabus will have been prepared by a conference which consists of four committees representing the LEA, the teachers, the Church of England, other Christian denominations and other faiths. Invitations to join this last committee come from the LEA and should be received by the denominations and faith groups in the area. In Wales there are only three committees, as there is no separate committee representing the Anglican Church.

There should be no difficulty for local churches to find out what is expected of them by this syllabus as they seek to support work in schools. They are likely to have had a representative of their own denomination on the conference. That person or a representative of the LEA should be able to answer questions about the syllabus and how churches can help schools implement it.

Churches that are asked to undertake work with a school or class need to ensure that they understand how the work they will do fits into the syllabus being used by the school.

An essential part of every school religious education programme will be the requirement to offer opportunities for children to learn about Christianity as it is experienced today in the Christian churches (Brown, 1994). Therefore it will be important for church members and particularly members of their ministerial teams to be prepared to visit schools to talk about what they believe and how it affects their lives. Sometimes these visitors will be clergy but schools will also wish to call upon 'ordinary' Christians as well. Local churches can help by being willing to suggest suitable local people. Schools will wish to invite clergy in to talk about their work and in some cases to talk about their role in leading worship including, where appropriate, the vestments that they wear.

Teaching and supporting religious education

In many churches where there is a paid priest or minister, they may feel that, as specialists in religious matters, they should be asked to make a larger contribution than this to the teaching of religious education in schools. Some clergy may expect to be invited to contribute to teaching about the Bible or the story of Christianity. In many primary schools, however, religious education will be integrated into the main timetable, and it should relate to the other topics that are being studied in the classroom. This may make it difficult to come in from outside to take this subject on its own. Not all priests or ministers will feel confident in their ability to teach young children, and so may be reluctant to become involved with these age groups. Taking a lesson or a series of lessons may not be the most useful contribution that a Christian minister can offer to a school. The development of school policies based on locally determined syllabuses can be a daunting task for a primary school. Few primary schools are able to recruit specialists in religious education, and to receive help from a local priest or minister, can be of considerable benefit in the task of developing school policies. This help will be more welcome when the priest or minister is able to offer insights as a trained theologian in a way that shows respect for the professionalism and integrity of the teachers.

In many secondary schools there will a specialist teacher of religious education. In such cases he or she will be better qualified professionally to teach the subject than most local priests or ministers. The subject specialist may, however, need help and support in two distinct areas.

1   The demands of the timetable on specialist teachers of religious education can often be very high. Not only may they be teaching a full timetable and seeing perhaps 500 pupils in a week, but they may also be supporting non-specialist colleagues who are contributing to the work of the department.

2.   As the lone specialist, they may find the demands made on them to promote the subject in the school and to maintain its position within the budget, timetable or examinations programme, difficult to meet in the long term.

The support of local ministers or priests whose academic background may be similar to their own can be encouraging and enabling for such teachers. For all these reasons it may be that for many priests or ministers the contribution to religious education could best be made in the staffroom or with the headteacher, during discussions about the teaching of the subject, rather than in the classroom.

Receiving visits

As part of their RE programme schools will wish to arrange visits to local places of worship in order to see what the worshipping community does (other types of visit to local churches will be dealt with in later sections). Therefore it will be important for churches to be prepared to welcome school parties to their church. Many dioceses have produced publications about school visits to churches like *Welcoming Schools*[4] and *Reaching Children*.[5]

Members of the ministerial team have a particularly important role to play in all of this but they should not ignore the potential for other members of the congregation to contribute. There may be some who can talk simply and well to children or teenagers about the church, what happens within it and why it is important to them.

A checklist for churches preparing for school visits

General

- Hold a planning meeting with representatives of the school to ensure that the purpose of the visit is clear and agreed.
- Ensure that there is a welcoming individual or group and that they are properly briefed.
- Ensure that the church is clean and warm for the visit.
- If there are areas that pupils are not allowed to enter are these clearly and appropriately marked?
- Are the locations of the nearest toilets clearly marked and known to the welcome party and the teachers?
- If there are pictures of saints or heroes of the faith, are their stories known to the welcome party? Are there cards available telling the stories in simple language?
- Do the church noticeboards communicate clearly how the church is involved in the local community and linked to other churches regionally, nationally and worldwide?
- If there is significant use of symbols within the church building, are their meanings known to the welcome party? Are there cards available giving their meanings?

Specific

- How can we present the church as a lively place of worship Sunday by Sunday?
- How can we present the way in which the church celebrates its special festivals?
- How can we present the way in which the church conducts baptisms, weddings and funerals?
- If the pupils are using worksheets, is the content known to the welcome group? Who has responsibility for the preparation of the worksheets?

The national curriculum subjects

The advent and continuing development of the national curriculum create a
need for schools to be able to call on adults with particular experience or skill
to supplement the educational provision for the children (Dearing, 1993).
As a result, a range of areas exists in which the churches may be able to provide
assistance beyond the field of religious education.

This opportunity to support schools may be particularly important in smaller
primary schools or in areas where community resources are difficult to identify
and use. The range of possible contributions is almost infinite, dependent as they
are only on the limitations of the experience and talents that are available inside
the church community. In one place the schools may gain assistance with the
computer or chess club, in another extra volunteers to assist on school trips,
in yet another someone to contribute to projects or to use their experience in
publishing the parish magazine to help the children publish one for their class or
school. These activities may not involve members of the ministerial team directly;
the only contact may be between the school and the member of the congregation
who has the skills and the time the school needs.

> The children were building a model of a working sailing boat, not a yacht.
> The children and their teacher had carefully and lovingly constructed it.
> The hull and mast were of wood and the model, five feet long, was almost
> complete, only the sails remained to be made. These were constructed of
> paper and carefully glued into place. They looked quite good. One of the
> sidesmen at the local church was a former fisherman. Visiting the school
> one day he saw the model. 'Its very good,' he said, ' but the rigging is not
> quite right and it is a pity that the sails are wrong.' The discussion with the
> children produced an offer to help. New rigging was constructed and sails
> were sewn from appropriate cloth. During the work, the fisherman's
> memory was picked clean of stories about fishing and the work done by
> boats like the one on which the model was based. For some years the
> model was a treasured item in the school, as a result of the stories
> associated with it.

While contributions towards the school's teaching programme can help the
school, they also create the opportunity for members of church ministerial teams
and others to establish good relationships with the children.

Some specific subject areas

Music

There is much good music teaching being provided in schools. Many parents are paying for their children to receive private instrumental lessons. Many churches are using a wide range of talents to provide the music for worship and for other activities. These different opportunities to learn music and to practise music-making are, in reality, interdependent. It is surprising, therefore, how often school and church seem to operate in ignorance of the work the other is doing. There are many opportunities to build on each other's work if only those involved in church music-making and music-making in school could develop better contacts. This is particularly true of instrumental music-making where churches may often be providing experience for children and young people of making music in company with adults, which is potentially very useful in their musical education. Good contacts between school and church could ensure that pupils know that the full range of their music-making is supported in both places.

While it may be that the church is using the school's training when it comes to instrumental music, the school may often be benefiting from the experience gained by children from singing in church choirs or music groups. Some schools may be fortunate in having a number of children in their classes who are learning to read music through singing in a local church choir and who can therefore form a comparatively skilled backbone in the school choir.

Cooperation between the churches and Church schools in the selection of a proportion of the songs and hymns used in worship can greatly enhance the benefits that children gain in their musical education from the work of both school and church. It will also provide important links between the worship happening in each place. This can be most clearly achieved where both places have one of their sources of hymns in common.

For many schools a visit to a church for any curriculum reason may be enhanced by a musical element. The opportunities for pupils to sing or play an appropriate song may help them to remember the purpose for which the church was built. The opportunity for them to hear the pipe organ, if there is one in the church, and to watch the organist could be a very special experience for young children, particularly those struggling with the first stages of piano lessons.

History

Religious education is not the only subject on the school curriculum where churches may be asked to assist. Many churches are among the oldest buildings in their neighbourhood and may contain much evidence of local history or examples of how local people have been involved in national events. Schools may request the opportunity for a class to visit a local church as part of their work in history. It is important that those who will receive the pupils and teachers for this visit know precisely what the pupils will be wanting to study. There is little point in putting the altar frontals on display if the pupils need to spend all their time examining the memorials in the church and the gravestones outside it. If the church has members who are particularly interested and knowledgeable about the history of the building, here may be a golden opportunity to share their enthusiasm with the children.

The Arts

The children attending the local primary school were invited by the local church to design Christmas cards. The most interesting of the designs were printed, with proper acknowledgements, by the church as the front covers for their leaflets about their Christmas services.

A newly created worship centre needed a cross and matching candleholders for their worship table. The local secondary school was approached. The result of the approach was a simply designed, well made set appropriate to the context in which they were to be used. It formed part of a GCSE project and was subsequently used regularly in worship.

In the previous section it was pointed out that for a visit by pupils studying history there might be little point in going to the effort of displaying the altar frontals. For many schools their local churches may be amongst the nearest places where the local community's active involvement in the arts is demonstrated. Visits which have the sculpture, stained glass or architecture as their main focus may be much enhanced by being shown the altar frontals, kneelers or similar items, particularly if the person doing the showing is someone who is responsible for their care and maintenance, or who has had a hand in making some of it.

Other curriculum areas

Although three particular areas of the curriculum have been selected so far, there is hardly an area of the curriculum to which a visit to a church cannot contribute.

The use of literature, particularly poetry within worship is a clear point of contact with the English curriculum.

Every Christian church uses light as a symbol (Genesis 1.3, John 1.1–5). Some churches make much of this symbolism visual with extensive use of candles (Paschal candle, Christingles, etc). Others may have pictures that make use of light as a symbol for holiness or for Christ. This symbolic use of light within the Christian Church could provide a focus for the religious education component of a school theme on light, for which the starting point could be an investigation of some of the scientific properties of light.

The links with missionaries, the work of worldwide organizations like the Mothers' Union or Traidcraft, the historic or continuing links with other churches at home and abroad, may all represent starting points or points of contact for the geography curriculum.

The wilder parts of a graveyard may offer interesting opportunities for nature study, some churches have even had conservation centres and nature trails set up in parts of their churchyards.

The important question when a school is planning a visit to the local church for a group of children is 'on what do you wish this particular visit to focus?' There then needs to follow some careful planning and the involvement of the most appropriate church members in order to ensure that the visit is of maximum benefit to the children.

Pilgrimages

For some schools, part of their programme of work may include the organization of a 'pilgrimage' related to the spiritual and moral development of their pupils. This may arise from a historical or religious project on pilgrimages. If this is happening it will be helpful if, in the context of providing the focus for the journey, the receiving church could provide information or examples of pilgrimages undertaken by church members recently or historically. Some schools may be unaware of the examples in current church life of journeys undertaken for spiritual purposes. Some of these are:

● In Essex, an annual ecumenical pilgrimage to Bradwell. Similar examples will exist in other parts of the country. Local schools working on pilgrimages should be aware of this event in order to show that pilgrimage is not just an old-fashioned idea but still has meaning for Christians today.

- A church coach party to hear an evangelist or attend a praise service at a major venue.

- A group from the church attending confirmation or ordination services at a cathedral.

- Visits by church members or church groups to the Holy Land or other important Christian sites.

- Journeys undertaken by representatives of the church to attend a service to mark the commencement of a new stage of ministry of a former leader.

Special events

There are special events in the life of both schools and churches that can bring them together. Sometimes these happen at the initiative of the local church, at other times it will be the school that makes the first move. Some examples are:

- A Suffolk church with a tradition of inviting the local county primary school to attend a service annually on the festival of the saint after whom the church is named. At the end of the service each child attending receives a bun.

- Special services, which are becoming increasingly common, to mark the move of a group of children from one stage of schooling to another or from school to higher education or work. Such services are important parts of these educational 'rites of passage'. Churches can help by providing venues or help in designing and preparing the services.

- At a recent schools event in a cathedral the focus was on the bells, which had recently been rehung after many years of silence. Those pupils attending the event took part in a range of workshops relating to the work of the cathedral, with several having an emphasis on the bells. In most dioceses cathedral events have tended to focus on the needs of Church schools, but, in one or two, there is now a growing demand from community schools for such events because they have heard such good reports of them from their colleagues in Church schools. An example of this is the Time Travellers project at Southwell Cathedral.

- In a number of secondary schools those responsible for the spiritual education of the pupils are offering to pupils the opportunity to go on retreat or for a quiet day. Churches that provide centres for such activities are clearly providing an important resource for such activity. Local ministerial teams should be aware of the retreat houses that are available and may be able to assist or support the planning of the programme for such events.

Voluntary societies

In many schools there is a range of voluntary societies and clubs that enhance the school's life and broaden the education of the children. Some of these, such as Christian Unions will be of obvious and direct interest to local churches. Others may only be sustained through the interest and expertise of local church people giving of their time to the school. The parish priest who helps with the football or the computer club or the minister who, with a teacher, runs a chess club in school are possible examples from a range that is as wide as the talents and interests of the local congregation.

Christian groups – a special case

Many schools, but not all, will have Christian clubs or meetings at lunchtime or after school. These are often run by staff and sometimes, in secondary schools, by older pupils. In many cases the staff involved will not be RE specialists, but will be practising Christians who teach other subjects. Such activities may only occasionally need physical help from local churches, but they should be a focus for encouragement, support and prayer by all the churches in the area.

Points for thought, discussion and action

What three activities from the range of possibilities suggested in this chapter could we, as a church, offer to local schools?

● What activities are we unable to help with?

● How could our people help?

● Are there activities that individuals in our church could offer to local schools?

---

9   *Pastoral issues*

> The headteacher should be able to look to the parish church as a
> source of unfailing support and encouragement.
>
> Recommendation from *The Way ahead*

> It should be a special objective of every Church school to engage
> the parents in the education and broader life of
> the child.
>
> Recommendation from *The Way ahead*

There will be times when, if good relations have been established between the
church ministerial team and the school, there can be fruitful sharing, cooperation
and joint work in the pastoral care of pupils, parents, staff and governors.

Pupils

All schools will be committed to providing a caring environment within which to
educate the children. At times this will lead them to undertake tasks that are not
strictly speaking part of a teacher's professional expertise. There may be trained
counsellors on the school staff, but even so most teachers and support workers,
as a result of the quality of their relationships with children, find themselves in
counselling roles without the benefits of appropriate training. In a large number
of schools there will be staff members who are also involved in supporting parents
through crises or periods of uncertainty. The demand for this support arises
partly out of the school's concern for the well-being of their pupils and partly
because, where parents trust the school, they may see it as the only source of
advice locally where the staff are on site (and therefore presumed to be available)
all day. Many teachers and headteachers feel inadequately trained for the role that
is expected of them. A discussion with a parent about why her daughter's work
seems to be suffering can rapidly change into what feels like a marriage guidance
session. It is pointless to say 'I am sorry, I am only concerned with her inability to
understand subtraction' when the parent is telling you that her daughter cannot
concentrate because she is worried that her father may be about to leave home.
Church ministerial team members can make a supportive contribution to this
work in several ways.

Prayer

Staff in schools need the prayerful support of local churches in all their work, but especially in their involvement in the care and support of children, young people and their families.

Support

Some church leaders may be able to develop relationships with the staff of the school to such an extent that they are able to provide some more direct support. In particular, they may be able to provide a listening ear for staff who have had to provide help to children or parents over problems that have been traumatic for individuals to discuss. Naturally, confidences must be respected but talking the issue over with someone who may have relevant experience and who is supportive can be extremely helpful.

Provision of resources

A number of churches publish material on aspects of pastoral care, which can be helpful to teachers and others in schools (e.g. Duffy, 1995). Teachers may not be aware of the existence of these resources, and members of ministerial teams may have an important role to play in drawing the attention of staff to these resources and the sources from which they may be obtained.

Direct involvement

This happens only very occasionally. When it does it will be the school making direct use of the pastoral skills of local church people with whom they have a good relationship. In such cases the church becomes one of the potential reference points when parents or children need more help than the school can give. Naturally, such references can only be made with the cooperation of the parent involved.

'Industrial chaplaincy' for pupils

Pupils also may need the opportunity to talk about their experience in school. This can lead to some delicate areas in church/school relations. Where problems emerge from such discussions, they are likely to be in one of three categories.

1. Concerns about progress, examination pressures, options and moves to the next stage of education.

2. Concerns about relationships with peers.

3. Concerns about relationships with staff.

Attentive listening, reassurance and encouragement are usually all that is needed. Rarely should action be promised or taken and certainly none should be considered that breaches confidence. Considerable sensitivity will be needed when a pupil's concerns reflect criticism of a member of the school staff with whom the listener is seeking to develop good working relationships.

Chapter 7 focused on the needs of teachers and the role of the church in providing 'industrial chaplaincy' for them. It will be clear that the chapter could also have formed an extended section of this one, but to save space and to avoid repetition no new material is included at this point.

'Industrial chaplaincy' for governors

Every school will have a significant number of governors. These are people who accept a major responsibility for the policies of the school and the appointment of the staff. They deserve the support of the churches in this voluntary work. Many of them will be a part of the local Christian community. Being a school governor is yet another way in which Christians can express their vocation to follow Christ by serving their local community. Christian governors may have a very important role to play in encouraging the links between the school and the local churches. This will not be their only task. They may be able to make an important contribution to the development of policy in religious education, school worship, sex education, and the spiritual, moral, social and cultural development of the pupils as well as areas of the general school curriculum where they have insights or expertise. They may also be able to support those parts of the school's management that are concerned with staff recruitment, selection, development and reward. They will bring important insights to bear on matters of pupil or even staff discipline. Governors are asked to contribute a considerable amount of their spare time to the role. It is important for churches to realize that one of the ways in which they can support members of their congregations who are governors is to free them from other commitments so that they can undertake this service.

Being a governor involves accepting responsibility for the formation of school policy and for the care, as employer, of the school staff. If a priest or minister accepts the role of governor, there may be times when these responsibilities may seem to conflict with any chaplaincy roles that the ministerial team may also be fulfilling in respect of the school. In such cases it may be important to share the duties between members of the ministerial team if this is possible. Indeed, in a number of Church schools the local ministers are breaking the tradition of accepting the chair of the governing body and supporting a lay member in that office in order to facilitate this. The duties of the parochial clergy in respect of the Church schools in their parish, including being ex officio a governor in many cases, are such that it is important that, when changes occur, new ministers are aware of the presence of a Church school or schools in the parish, and are positive in their commitment to them.

Parents

Parents, or those who have the parental responsibility for children in their care, have a major role to play in their children's education. This is not just limited to choosing the right schools and then supporting the work of that school. By the example that they provide they are major educators of their children in the home, and there is a limit to what can be achieved at school in areas where children have already learned negative attitudes to schools or learning from their parents. Among the possible examples of this is learning to read. A school can teach a child to read, but if there is no example of reading in the home then it will be much more difficult to enable the child to become a reader who enjoys books for information and entertainment.

Ideally, there should be a partnership between the parents and the school in the interest of the child, and much of the school's contact with parents will be designed to foster this partnership. Parents and schools do not always agree, but they should seek to reconcile their differences in order to ensure that their shared goals are achieved.

Christian parents

Christian parents have an important role in setting an example within the partnership between school and parents in general, and encouraging the school to meet its spiritual aims. This requires them to take a positive role in the affairs of the school that their children attend. The church should encourage them in this. Equally, the church may be taking initiatives to encourage Christian parents to think deeply about their role as a parent in the context of their beliefs. The churches may also be providing the support that parents need in the early years of children's lives through the provision of Parents and Toddler clubs and Playgroups. This support for Christian parents provided by the church's ministerial team will create natural links with schools in the area. Christian parents may be able to facilitate such links.

Christian parents will wish to ensure that the school they choose for their children is a good school in academic and pastoral terms. They will also wish to be certain that the spiritual dimension of the school, the religious education and the programme of school worship have been given a proper priority in the school's planning and are an important part of the daily life of the school. This should apply to all types of school, not just to Church schools, as these areas of school life are required by law. Therefore, when they read about or visit a school that they are considering for their children, they will look for what is said and done about the teaching of religious education and the national curriculum, school worship and the care of the children, as well as the quality of the art work, the number of cups on display, the behaviour and politeness of the children or the impressiveness of the examination results.

Points for thought, discussion and action

- What are we doing to support Christians in our congregation who are involved in local schools?

- What are we doing to support all those working in the schools in the area served by our church?

- How may our work with parents link with that of schools?

---

10   *Sharing activities*

> Many schools and churches provide human and other resources
> to engage pupils' interest and encourage them
> to think and reflect.

The Way ahead, para. 7.12

Communication

In any community there will be difficulties in ensuring that accurate information
is transmitted about the local community institutions. School-gate gossip can be
very spontaneous and misinformed. Too often letters carried home by children
are processed through the washing machine before parents read them. As a result
every school will be looking for ways in which to ensure that its communications
are improved. This has become even more important with the publication of
league tables of examination and test results. Schools need to develop means
whereby the local community knows sufficient about the school's total life to
place the league table results in context. Similarly, churches find it difficult to
overcome the barriers created by indifference or stereotyped views, when seeking
to inform the wider community of their work and activities. There is a clear case
for cooperation here.

> Each month the church magazine carries an item from one of the local
> schools. The item may be a report on the recent activities in the school.
> It may be some examples of work that the pupils have done. Each school
> takes it in turn to contribute so that it does not become a burden on a
> single school and there is always plenty of variety.

Churches should be able to find ways in which local schools can communicate
to church members. Exhibitions of work mounted as part of the focus on schools
provided by Education Sunday could be one example of this.

Schools could provide opportunities for the local church or churches to let
parents and children know about activities and services; churches could provide
opportunities for schools to let their congregations know about what the school
is doing. In many small communities this happens easily and naturally. In larger
urban communities it appears to be extremely difficult. Is this because there is
less mutual good will, or are people not allowing themselves sufficient time to
communicate with each other effectively?

Fund-raising

Churches and schools both need to raise funds to support their own activities over and above the contributions of regular members or funds received from the government or local authority. It is sensible to suggest that a minimum of cooperation and communication could avoid the worst of clashes and be of mutual assistance. Beyond liaison over the dates and places of events, more could easily be done. Mutual support through publicizing each other's activities is a simple and obvious place to start. The school might contribute items to the entertainment at the church fête or concert. The church might provide additional adults or the use of a hall for the school's fund-raising activities.

A further aspect of fund-raising that should be mentioned is the charitable giving that is undertaken by schools and by churches. Most schools seek to have a charitable project every term or year. Usually there is a school policy indicating how such projects are to be handled. Most churches have a policy that requires them to give a proportion of their income to charitable purposes outside the parish. Such activities could be mutually supporting. They are certainly activities where good communication could be mutually enhancing. Obvious examples of full cooperation include the school's making a collection to support the local church group that is taking a truckload of supplies to Romania, or the church's appealing for its members to help the children collect items to be sold to support famine relief work in Africa. It may even be that, on occasions, a church and school could agree to work together on a project.

Money management

When financial resources are tight and money has to be efficiently managed it is important that organizations respect each other's budgets. Schools should be sensitive to when they are expecting churches to support them financially. If, for instance, the school asks to borrow the local church for a concert, has a reasonable sum been offered to cover the costs involved in heating the church? By now churches should have adjusted to the impact of Local Financial Management on schools. Schools have full responsibility for their own budgets. Therefore it is not the LEA that is subsidizing the letting of the school hall for the church scout group, but the budget that should be spent on the provision of teachers or consumable materials in the classroom. It is important that churches are willing to pay a proper charge for the use of school premises.

This is not to suggest that every aspect of mutual cooperation should have its price or that every offer of payment will be accepted. Much can be achieved by mutual help and cooperation without financial issues being raised. It is important, however, that no one assumes that the other party has such well-developed sources of funding that it is unnecessary to consider the real cost of requests that are being made.

Contributing to the extension of facilities

Few schools or churches have all the plant and facilities that they need. In some places sharing arrangements, formal or informal, can greatly enhance the work done. Churches may be used by schools for acts of worship, concerts or as places to study aspects of religious education, local history or the arts. Schools may be used by churches to provide space for meetings, Sunday school classes or even acts of worship. Taking account of the comments in the financial management section, there seems to be no limit to the possibilities. In some places, schools and churches have worked together to provide playgroups or other facilities for the wider local community.

Meeting places

Since many schools do not have large spaces in which to hold meetings, perform or hold acts of worship, it is not uncommon for such schools to approach local churches with requests for help.

> Can we book the parish hall for a Parents' Association Dance?

> Could we hold the carol service in the church because so many parents will want to come that we cannot fit them all into the school hall? (In one church in east London there is a school carol service on almost every day of the last fortnight of the Christmas term, bringing over 2,000 local children and young people plus their parents into church. It is worth noting here that these visitors are coming to use the church for its prime purpose, the worship of God.)

These are opportunities for churches to make schools welcome, to work with them and to build good relationships. Of course, not every request can be met. Certainly some requests will involve costs that the school should be prepared to pay, but all such requests are opportunities for contact and mutual support.

Mutual support

There have already been examples in the preceding chapters of areas where the school may welcome contacts with the local churches for mutual support. Schools and churches that serve the same area should have a close relationship, if only to ensure that they are mutually informed about activities that are being planned or areas of shared concern. These concerns will vary according to local community circumstances. In one area it may be the pressures on family life caused by the local economic situation and the absence of a locally accessible DHSS office. In another it may be the problem of children being involved in so many activities in and out of school that careful coordination of plans is necessary in order to avoid clashes and the resulting distressed children and irate parents.

Points for thought, discussion and action

- Do we coordinate dates of fund-raising with our local schools?

- Do we seek mutual support for special efforts and appeals?

- Do we respect the school's budget when seeking to use their premises?

- Do they respect ours?

- How can we liaise over initiatives to meet local community needs?

---

11 What about Church schools?

> All parishes and all Church schools should reflect on the
> implications of the General Synod Resolution that Church
> schools are at the centre of the Church's mission in terms
> of their own parish and their own school.

Recommendation from *The Way ahead*

The publication, in 2001, of *The Way ahead* and its subsequent adoption by the
Church of England, has raised the profile of Church schools. It has also drawn
into the open a number of criticisms of the work of Church schools. Much of the
criticism is built on stereotypes that do not match the reality of work in Church
schools. Therefore it is important to provide a brief introduction to the work of
Church schools.

Strictly speaking, the schools that the Anglican tradition refers to as 'Church
schools' are a part of those schools in the maintained system that have a 'religious
character' (see Chapter 17).

The Church of England has a long history of involvement with schools in the
maintained system of education as well as schools in the independent sector.
There are currently 4,700 Church of England schools and 184 Church in Wales
schools. In England 925,890 pupils attend Church of England schools, which is
12.4 per cent of all pupils in the maintained system in this country. Most of these
schools are primary serving the age range from four to eleven but there are also a
number of secondary schools. There are over 43,017 teachers and 70,000 school
governors engaged in providing the education in these schools supported by the
Diocesan Directors of Education and their teams. Some of these schools have a
long tradition, while others are quite recently founded, but most probably have
their roots in the last century, even if they are now in modern buildings. Some
Church schools have a tradition of serving the Christian community by giving
priority in their admissions to the children of church members; others serve their
geographical community by giving priority to the children living close to the
school, others seek to combine both these traditions in their admission policies.
The Roman Catholic Church has over 2,104 schools serving 719,804 pupils or
9.6 per cent of children in the maintained system in England. There are 35,764
teachers and approximately 25,000 governors in Roman Catholic schools in the
maintained sector. The diocesan teams for schools and for religious education
support them.

The Methodist Church has 28 schools in the maintained system serving 5,018 pupils or under 0.1 per cent of the children in the maintained system.

A small but growing number of Church schools are ecumenical in their foundation, being funded jointly by more than one Church or by independent Christian trusts. There are 74 schools of this type in the maintained system serving 32,105 pupils or 0.4 per cent of all children in the maintained system. These schools employ 1,750 teachers and have approximately 500 governors.

Every Church school represents a considerable commitment in time and money on behalf of the local church community to enable it to continue in existence. Such a commitment is rewarded by the pastoral contacts that it provides for the church with the children and their parents and into the wider community and the opportunity that it gives to influence by example the work done in other schools in the area. The benefit to the parish of having a church school has been demonstrated by recent research findings (Francis and Lankshear, 2001). The appreciation of the role of the Churches and their schools in the education system of this country by the government is demonstrated by reference to it in the recent White Paper (HMSO, 2001).

How do Church schools provide Christian witness?

Church schools provide a witness to Christ by the quality of the service they provide to the community and the way in which they make clear their motivation for this. Therefore, it is important that they are good schools, and that no one can be in any doubt that they are Church schools. Such schools will demonstrate that they have a clear understanding of what it means to be the Church school in the location in which it is set (Brown and Lankshear, 2000). This implies that the worship and the religious education are excellent and that the relationships within the school, and between the school and members of the wider community, are founded on the teaching of the Gospels (Lankshear, 2000). At a more mundane level, there should be clear signals in the school and outside it that this is a church school. No one should be left in any doubt on that score. This does not mean that there should not be sensitivity to and respect for the feelings of parents and pupils from other faiths, but rather than such sensitivity should not involve a Church school in apologizing for its Christian foundation.

The worshipping community and the Church school

The worshipping community that has a Church school has an important privilege and responsibility. It benefits from the opportunities that the school provides to show its care and concern for the people living in the parish through the provision of high quality education for the children, and through the opportunities for contact that the existence of the school creates. Of course, there are costs in terms of money and time, and it is to be hoped that neighbouring churches will wish to be helpful and supportive in meeting such costs, but the potential rewards in the long term outweigh the short-term problems. In many parishes the school buildings also represent a major asset in the church's pastoral and social work outside school hours where this is compatible with the primary purpose of the building, which is the provision of education in a school context. Support for the school should be more than worship. Finance, prayer, time and talents need to be committed in this great work of education.

Churches that have Church schools have a particular range of tasks that need to be undertaken in support of them (Lankshear, 2000). These include:

a.   Chaplaincy: supporting the pupils and staff of the school and contributing to the worshipping life of the school and its Christian ethos.

b.   Governance: providing a number of people, including the priest or minister, to be members of the governing body whose work includes all aspects of:

   – employing staff
   – developing policies
   – managing finance and buildings
   – possibly administering admissions
   – aspects of the school's discipline procedures.

c.   Funding: most churches will contribute to the costs of supporting the school on a regular basis, including making provision in their budgets for regular donations. In all Church schools this will provide some finance to support the aspect of the Christian character of the school. In voluntary aided schools it will also contribute to the governing body's share of the costs related to the school premises.

d.   Work with parents: being involved with the Parent/Teacher Association or its equivalent and knowing parents and their children so that the school may be assisted to respond to their needs.

e.   Being involved in community and LEA networks, i.e. governor training activities, LEA Officers, etc.

f.   The parish priest and some of the lay officials of the church may be involved as trustees of the school building and any money or other property held on trust for the school.

The priest/minister cannot do all of this. He or she will need help and support, for every church with a Church school there needs to be careful prayer and thought before it is decided what tasks the priest/minister will undertake and what will be done by other church members. There are no rules here, except that it is very rare for the priest/minister not to be on the governing body. Tradition only helps if it helps. In many Church schools the priest/minister is the chair of the governing body. This is tradition. It is helpful if one of the church governors is the chair but it should only be the priest if that is the best use of everyone's time and talents.

For most churches that have a Church school there will be at least five or six church members, including the priest or minister, who are giving significant time to support the school. They in their turn need support from the church.

From time to time the Church Council will have business to conduct in relation to the school. They cannot do this effectively if they never hear about the school at other times. There should exist well developed ways for the council to hear about the activities of the school and the governors via reports or items for discussion. This will ensure that, for example, when the Church Council receives a copy of an inspection report from OFSTED on the work of the Church school they will have a basis of knowledge and understanding on which to receive it.

One way of establishing such links is for the headteacher of the school to be an ex officio member of the PCC. In some areas, when a new headteacher is appointed to work in a Church school, the church holds a special service to commission the headteacher to this Christian ministry.

Points for thought, discussion and action

● Are there Church schools in the area served by this church?
● At what cost, financial and human, is the church's involvement being maintained?
● How can we help?

---

12 Regional and national levels of support

The (Archbishops') Council should lead the Church in considering afresh how all elements of the Church – parishes, schools, diocese, Church Colleges and Theological Colleges, courses and schemes – can work more closely together in true partnership . . .

Recommendation from *The Way ahead*

It should not be forgotten that many Churches have regional and national organizations that are active in education. Regionally, the Anglican and Catholic dioceses are active in their support of work in schools, and many other denominations will have resources available at this level.

Sometimes ecumenical organizations are able to sponsor schools workers for an area, perhaps working with the support of Scripture Union or another similar agency. Where such workers exist it is important that their brief is clear and that they are enabled to relate effectively to other Christians already involved with the schools locally or regionally. Their tasks need to be carefully defined. Requiring them to relate to schools within several of the models of work mentioned in Chapter 2 may lead to confusion or disappointment when assumed objectives are not met.

Nationally, in the Church of England, the Board of Education and the National Society are the means whereby the support for the work of Church schools, religious education, school worship and Christian teachers are resourced and given a focus. The Catholic Education Service does equivalent work for the Roman Catholic Church in England and Wales. Other denominations have their own structures and these meet together nationally through the Churches' Joint Education Policy Committee (CJEPC), which is related to Christians Together in England. Ecumenical bodies that work to support schools include Scripture Union and the Christian Education Movement.

A particular national initiative supported by the CJEPC, which can help local churches in their work with schools, is Education Sunday. This takes place every year on the ninth Sunday before Easter. Materials for the event are developed ecumenically but published by individual denominations in ways that are appropriate to their own traditions. It provides an opportunity to celebrate and pray for the work of schools and colleges. It can be an opportunity to make the whole congregation aware of the close relationships that have been developed between the churches and local schools.

Further information can be obtained from The National Society or on the web site www.natsoc.org.uk.

No local church should be unaware of how its own denomination, or the churches working ecumenically, support work in schools. However, it is the role of the local church in supporting Christians involved with education that is of vital importance if the church is to continue to make a full contribution to the education system into the next century. It is a task for every church, even if there is no Church school and no teacher, governor, educational administrator or even child in the congregation. Prayer is important; practical and moral support are important; financial support is important – and every church can give these.

Points for thought, discussion and action

- Do we know what our church is doing at regional and national level in education?

- How are we making this work known to local schools?

- Is there a local schools worker?

- Do we know what this worker is attempting?

- How are we supporting this work?

---

13   *No one can do everything*

> Governing bodies should be vigilant to see that the headteachers
> in small schools do not exhaust themselves
> by taking on a greater teaching load than they should . . .
>
> Recommendation from *The Way ahead*

(Author's note: Their advice goes beyond headteachers in small
schools. All involved in or with schools have to guard against the
danger of over committing themselves.)

In the last section, a range of possible ideas for action were explored. No church
acting on its own could possibly do everything. No school would want all these
things done. Choices have to be made between possibilities. Most of these will
be determined by local factors

- What are the pressing needs?
- Where do our talents lie?
- What resources do we have available?

Some choices will be made because they are simple, obvious and essential.
These form a basic minimum, which the churches in an area, acting together,
should be able to provide for every school.

The minimum action kit was discussed in detail in Chapter 6. The main
headings were:

- Prayer
- Befriending
- Positive concern/support
- Welcome ministry
- Freeing members for ministry.

No church that is doing all these things should feel guilty if it is not doing more.
More may be possible and desirable but only where resources, people and time
(not necessarily money) permit. If there is to be only one of these five, then it
must be prayer. If there is prayer it is unlikely that, in time, it will be the only one.

Working in the service of local schools should not be a chore or a duty – it should be a joy and a privilege. It is so exciting to be involved in helping children and young people to grow and learn that no one should begrudge being involved. Of course there are frustrations. Children are not perfect. Young people can be and often are adolescent in all the negative meanings of that word. There are, however, also joys – sharing in the successes of individuals and schools, the laughter when things go right or when they end in spectacular failure. The joys outweigh the frustrations. We know that we are serving Christ in serving schools and the pupils in them. What greater joy could there be than that?

Part 4

Resources and further information

14   Commissioning services

Using this liturgy is one of the ways in which teaching and learning can be supported and celebrated in your community. Teaching and learning take place in many different ways and in a variety of settings and so the following framework has been designed to be adaptable. It could, for example, form part of an order of service, following the sermon and ending with the Peace. The second service is most appropriate for an individual or for a group taking on a new task or beginning a new job.

It could be used at the start of a new year or within a Eucharist for all the staff of the school at the beginning of a new term.

The first service is appropriate for all those working in education and is probably most appropriate as part of an Education Sunday service or in the context of public worship on the Sunday before the start of a new school year.

The term 'teacher' is intended in its broadest sense to include those involved in working with people of all ages.

The services may be photocopied. They are also available to download for free from The National Society's website, www.natsoc.org.uk.

A service of rededication

Invocation

Leader: After three days they found Jesus in the temple, sitting among the teachers, listening to them and asking them questions. (Luke 2.46)

Profession of Faith

The leader invites all gathered to profess the faith of the Church

Leader: Do you believe and trust in God the Father,
who made all things?

All: **We believe and trust in him.**

Leader: Do you believe and trust in his Son Jesus Christ,
who redeemed the world?

All: **We believe and trust in him.**

Leader: Do you believe and trust in his Holy Spirit,
who gives life to the people of God?

All: **We believe and trust in him.**

Leader: This is the faith of the Church.

All: **This is our faith.**
We believe and trust in one God,
Father, Son and Holy Spirit. Amen

Commission

The leader invites teachers to stand or to come forward

Leader: Lord Jesus Christ, the source of all knowledge and truth, give to all who teach, wisdom, strength and compassion in all they undertake,

and grant that all who learn may be open to your transforming
power; for your sake.

All: **Amen.**

Leader: The Lord is our teacher.
Will you promise to offer all those you serve a vision of life
inspired by the example of Jesus?

Teachers: **With God's help, we will.**

Leader: As Christians we are required to promote the values of the
kingdom of God.
Will you foster justice and equality within our community?

Teachers: **With God's help, we will.**

Leader: Will you strive to offer, by word and deed, a Christian example
to those you serve in our community?

Teachers: **With God's help, we will.**

The leader addresses all present and invites them to stand

Leader: As part of our mission and ministry,
we are all called by God, to teach and to learn together
Will you pray regularly for each other as learners and teachers?

All: **With God's help, we will.**

Leader: In recognition of our calling, we all say together:

All: **In darkness and in light,
in trouble and in joy,
help us, heavenly Father,
to trust your love
to serve your purpose,
and to praise your name,
through Jesus Christ our Lord. Amen.**

Teachers return to their seats

Intercessions

Leader: God of all time and wisdom, through the power of your Spirit,
enlighten us all as we teach and as we learn,
that we may discern your word and find your truth.

Lord, by your Spirit:

All: **Bring in your kingdom.**

Leader: God our inspiration, uphold all those who exercise their vocation
in education whether as teachers, leaders or helpers.
In our community we pray for . . .

Lord, by your Spirit:

All: **Bring in your kingdom.**

Leader: God our anchor and support, we pray for all those who are
responsible for education planning, policy making and
administration. In our community we pray for . . .

Lord, by your Spirit:

All: **Bring in your kingdom.**

Leader: God of healing and wholeness, we give thanks for all the
educational opportunities made available to us. Protect and sustain
all those who are denied access to education or training.
In our community we pray for . . .

Lord, by your Spirit:

All: **Bring in your kingdom.**

Leader: God of renewal and growth, give us all, learners and teachers,
children and adults, ears that are eager to listen, eyes that are quick
to see, hands that are sure to do, and hearts that are always open to
learn more of your love.
Lord of the Church

All: **Hear our prayer,**
and make us one in heart and mind
to serve you with joy forever. *Amen.*

The Peace is then shared

A service of commitment – for an individual being commissioned to a specific post

Invocation

Leader: After three days they found Jesus in the temple, sitting among the teachers, listening to them and asking them questions. (Luke 2.46)

Profession of Faith

The leader invites all gathered to profess the faith of the Church

Leader: Do you believe and trust in God the Father, who made all things?

All: **We believe and trust in him.**

Leader: Do you believe and trust in his Son Jesus Christ, who redeemed the world?

All: **We believe and trust in him.**

Leader: Do you believe and trust in his Holy Spirit, who gives life to the people of God?

All: **We believe and trust in him.**

Leader: This is the faith of the Church.

All: **This is our faith.**
        We believe and trust in one God,
        Father, Son and Holy Spirit. *Amen*

Commission

The leader invites the headteacher/teacher to be commissioned and his/her colleagues stand or to come forward

Leader: Lord Jesus Christ, the source of all knowledge and truth, give to all who teach, wisdom, strength and compassion in all they undertake, and grant that all who learn may be open to your transforming power; for your sake.

All: **Amen.**

The leader addresses the headteacher/teacher to be commissioned

Leader: . . . you have been called by God to serve as . . . in . . . School.

Will you faithfully serve the pupils in the school in the name of Jesus Christ?

Headteacher: **With God's help, I will.**

The leader addresses the headteacher/teacher's colleagues

Leader: . . . will share in your work of Christian service. Will you support . . . in his/her task by your prayer, in working together and in fellowship?

Colleagues: **With God's help, we will.**

Leader: The Lord is our teacher. Will you promise to offer all those you serve a vision of life inspired by the example of Jesus?

Colleagues: **With God's help, we will.**

Leader: Will you encourage all to follow Jesus' commandment to love one another?

Colleagues: **With God's help, we will.**

Leader: As Christians we are required to promote the values of the Kingdom of God.
Will you foster justice and equality within our community?

Colleagues: **With God's help, we will.**

Leader: Will you foster respect for all God's creation?

Colleagues: **With God's help, we will.**

Leader:: Will you strive to offer, by word and deed, a Christian example to those you serve in our community?

Colleagues: **With God's help, we will**.

The leader addresses all present and invites them to stand

Leader: As part of our mission and ministry, we are all called by God, to teach and to learn together. Will you pray regularly for each other as learners and teachers?

All: **With God's help, we will**.

Leader: In recognition of our calling, we all say together:

All: **In darkness and in light,**
in trouble and in joy,
help us, heavenly Father,
to trust your love
to serve your purpose,
and to praise your name,
through Jesus Christ our Lord. *Amen.*

For a teacher being commissioned a candle or other gift could be presented to mark the occasion.

For a commissioning of a headteacher the following pattern of welcomes and gifts could be used.

Incumbent:

. . . to be entrusted with the leadership and management of a Church school and the nurture of its pupils is a solemn trust. We pray that God will strengthen you, by his grace, faithfully to fulfil this task.

Churchwardens:

On behalf of the Trustees and the local congregation we affirm you. We present you with the keys of N School as a symbol of your affirmation in headship. May God bless you in all that you do.

Diocesan representative:
> On behalf of the Chairman and Board of Education of the Diocese of . . . , receive this Bible to mark your affirmation in headship. It is God's word and the foundation of all true wisdom. Use it to guide and inspire you.

Local Education Authority Officer:
> On behalf of the Chairman and Board of Education of the County of . . . , receive this gift to mark your headship. It is a symbol of our partnership and support in your continuing work in this community.

Teachers return to their seats

Intercessions

Leader:
> God of all time and wisdom, through the power of your Spirit, enlighten us all as we teach and as we learn, that we may discern your word and find your truth.
>
> Lord, by your Spirit:

All: **Bring in your kingdom.**

Leader:
> God our inspiration, uphold all those who exercise their vocation in education whether as teachers, leaders or helpers. In our community we pray for . . .
>
> Lord, by your Spirit:

All: **Bring in your kingdom.**

Leader:
> God our anchor and support, we pray for all those who are responsible for education planning, policy making and administration. In our community we pray for . . .
>
> Lord, by your Spirit:

All: **Bring in your kingdom.**

Leader:	God of healing and wholeness, we give thanks for all the educational opportunities made available to us. Protect and sustain all those who are denied access to education or training. In our community we pray for . . .
	Lord, by your Spirit:
All:	**Bring in your kingdom.**
Leader:	God of renewal and growth, give us all, learners and teachers, children and adults, ears that are eager to listen, eyes that are quick to see, hands that are sure to do, and hearts that are always open to learn more of your love.
All:	**Lord of the Church** **hear our prayer** **and make us one in heart and mind** **to serve you with joy forever. Amen.**

The Peace is then shared

15 Prayers for teachers and schools

Valuing teachers and responding to or supporting their vocation includes choosing prayers that reflect their needs. The following short collection of prayers, drawn from a number of sources, provides a starting point for selecting prayers that can be used in a liturgical context.

Prayers for vocation

Almighty God,
you have entrusted to your Church
a share in the ministry of your Son our great high priest:
inspire by your Holy Spirit the hearts of many
to offer themselves for the ministry of your Church,
that strengthened by his power,
they may work for the increase of your kingdom
and set forward the eternal praise of your name;
through Jesus Christ your Son our Lord.

(For Vocations, *Common Worship*, p. 105)

Almighty and everlasting God,
by whose Spirit the whole body of the Church
is governed and sanctified:
hear our prayer which we offer or all your faithful people;
that each in his vocation and ministry
may serve you in holiness and truth
to the glory of your name;
through our Lord and Saviour Jesus Christ.

(Vocations to Religious Communities, *The Alternative Service Book 1980*, p. 967)

Almighty God
you have enlightened your Church
by the teaching of your servant N.
Enrich it evermore with your heavenly grace,
and raise up faithful witnesses,

who by their life and teaching
may proclaim to all men the truth of your salvation;
through Jesus Christ our Lord.

(Of a Teacher of the Faith or Confessor, *The Alternative Service Book 1980,* p. 849.)

Almighty and merciful God, of whose only gift it cometh that thy faithful people
do unto thee true and laudable service; Grant, we beseech thee, that we may so
faithfully serve thee in this life, that we fail not finally to attain thy heavenly
promises; through the merits of Jesus Christ our Lord. Amen.

(The Collect, The Thirteenth Sunday after Trinity, *The Book of Common Prayer,*
p. 201)

Almighty God, who by thy Divine Providence hast appointed divers Orders
of Ministers in thy Church, and didst inspire thine Apostles to choose into the
Order of Deacons the first Martyr Saint Stephen, with others; Mercifully behold
these thy servants now called to the like Office and Administration; replenish
them so with the truth of thy Doctrine, and adorn them with innocency of life,
that, both by word and good example, they may faithfully serve thee in this
Office, to the glory of thy Name, and the edification of thy Church; through
the merits of our Saviour Jesus Christ, who liveth and reigneth with thee and
the Holy Ghost, now and for ever. Amen.

(The Collect, The Ordering of Deacons, *The Book of Common Prayer,* p. 642)

Prayers and blessings to be used in school

Inside this school, O Lord, there are lots of people
trying to know and understand your world.
Give us courage when things are difficult,
hope when things seem gloomy
and joy when things go well.
Amen.

Let thy blessing, O Lord,
rest upon our work in this school.
Teach us to seek after truth

and enable us to attain it;
and grant that
as we increase in knowledge of earthly things,
we may grow in knowledge of thee,
whom to know is life eternal;
through Jesus Christ our Lord.
Amen.

(Adapted from Thomas Arnold, 1795–1842, of Rugby School)

Lord, let your Holy Spirit rest upon our school
that it may be a place of love and truth
where the weak are made strong,
and the strong learn humility,
and all of us learn the wisdom
that alone comes from you.
Amen.

God bless our school;
bless those who teach,
bless those who learn,
and bless us all with the knowledge of your love;
through Jesus Christ our Lord.
Amen.

Holy and loving God;
open our eyes to see you,
open our minds to trust you,
open our hearts to love you
this day and for evermore.
Amen.

Father of love, make us like gleaming mirrors
so that we may reflect your marvellous light.
Amen.

(Taken from 'School', Herbert, 1993b, pp. 133–5.)

Father, we thank you for your blessing on this school, and for the love and labour of all who have made it a house of faith and of fruitful study. Grant that we in our turn may follow their example, and may so learn truth as to bear its light along all our ways, and so learn Christ as ever to be found in him.

(King's College, Cambridge)

(Taken from 'Prayers for Young People', David Foster (ed.), 1999.)

Holy Spirit, coming so silently,
giving life and refreshment and beauty
everywhere;
coming in a way none can understand;
coming invisibly;
coming in the night of affliction;
may your peace dwell in my heart,
may your strength invigorate me,
may your love kindle my whole being,
to love him who first loved me.

Lord, whether I am good or bad
I am always yours.
If you won't have me, who will?
If you take no notice, who will care for me?
Your forgiveness far outweighs my wickedness;
your love is much deeper than the depth of my sin.
Lord, whatever kind of person I am,
I am always yours.

(J. M. Neale, 1818–1866)

('Self-Offering', taken from Herbert, 1993a, p. 72.)

16 The Church's year and the school year

Church season	School year
Advent	Carol services
	Nativity plays
	Christmas parties
Christmas	Holiday
Epiphany	Epiphany services
	Return to school
Candlemas	Special services
Septuagesima (Ninth Sunday before Easter – Education Sunday)	Taking part in special events in church
Lent	Pancake day party
	Ash Wednesday service
	Lent activities
	Staff 'appointing season' begins
Easter	Holiday
	SATS
	GCSEs begin
	AS and A levels begin
Ascension	Special services
	Staff 'appointing season' ends (31 May)
Pentecost	Special services
Summer holidays	Holidays
	GCSE/AS/A level results
	New school year
	New teachers start careers
Harvest	Special services
All Saints/All Souls	Some schools celebrate Hallowe'en
	Some schools celebrate All Saints

17　The different types of school

The descriptions given below are short and do not do justice to the particular types of school, but it is hoped that they will stimulate church people to find out more. All the statistics reflect the position in January 2001 and are taken from the relevant Department for Education and Skills statistical tables or from detailed work done by the Church of England Board of Education team.

a. The maintained system

This includes all schools that are part of the state system of education; that is they receive their financing from the state and education in them is free, although parents and the local community may help to raise money for the school. Within the maintained system, schools may only charge for activities that are not part of the 'curriculum' of the school. There are 21,550 maintained schools in England. These schools provide education for 7,804,866 pupils.

Voluntary: A school within the maintained system which is owned or administered by an educational trust. Most trusts are religious but some may derive from secular bodies such as the City Livery Companies. Voluntary schools are part of the school system that is the responsibility of LEAs. Almost one-third of all schools in the maintained system are voluntary schools. Of these the majority are Anglican and most of the remainder are Roman Catholic. Some aspects of all voluntary schools must be conducted in accordance with the Trust Deed of the school. There are 7,054 voluntary schools in England (33 per cent of all maintained schools). They provide education for 1,827,051 pupils (23.4 per cent of those in the maintained system).

Community: A school in the maintained system which is not a voluntary or foundation school and for which the LEA is responsible. There are 13,642 community schools in England.

Voluntary aided: A voluntary school in which the governing body is responsible for the capital costs of the building and any improvement to it. They receive grant from the Department for Education and Skills towards the cost of this work. The LEA makes all other payments. The governing body is the legal employer of most of the staff and are responsible for the admissions policy of the school. Religious education and school worship are conducted in accordance with the school's trust deed. The foundation governors, that is those representing the church, faith group or other trust, have an absolute majority over all other groups of governor.

There are 4,274 aided schools in England (19.8 per cent of all maintained schools).

Voluntary controlled: A voluntary school in which the governing body does not provide any financial contribution to the maintenance of the building. The school, while retaining certain aspects of the voluntary school, is controlled by the LEA, who employs the staff and is responsible for the admission policy of the school. Worship in a controlled school must be conducted in accordance with the school Trust Deed. The foundation governors form one group on the governing body, but no group has a majority. There are 2,780 Controlled schools in England (12.9 per cent of all maintained schools).

Foundation schools: These schools share many of the characteristics of voluntary schools. Like voluntary aided schools, the governing bodies of these schools are the employers of the staff and control the admissions to the school. Like Voluntary Controlled schools the LEA is responsible for all funding. The requirements for religious education and school worship also follow the pattern for a voluntary controlled school. There is no single group of governors with an absolute majority. There are 854 foundation schools in England (4 per cent of all maintained schools).

City Technology Colleges: These schools were created to stimulate the development of high quality science and technology teaching. They receive a proportion of their funds direct from central government but they also have sponsors who have contributed significantly to their initial costs. The sponsors are usually industrial companies. There are 15 City Technology Colleges in England.

Comprehensive: This is a description usually applied to secondary schools that take in children from the entire ability range. Sometimes they may exist alongside grammar schools and therefore only attract a reduced proportion of children with the highest academic ability. Normally they need to be quite large schools in order to be able to provide a range of courses suitable for all abilities. Of all secondary age pupils in maintained schools, 87 per cent attend a comprehensive school.

Grammar: These schools select the most academically able children from the area that they serve. The courses provided in them are then designed to enable the selected children to achieve the highest standards of which they are capable. Traditionally these schools served between 10 and 15 per cent of the population. In some areas where only a few grammar schools have been retained these schools may only be serving the top 2 per cent of the ability range. In many areas they no longer exist. Of all secondary age pupils in maintained schools, 4.4 per cent attend a grammar school.

Modern: These schools provide secondary education for pupils who are not selected for grammar school education in areas where grammar schools take a significant proportion of the total school population. In a few of these areas there may also be **Technical schools,** which provide a technically orientated education for pupils whose abilities suggest that type of education would be appropriate. Of all secondary age pupils in maintained schools, 4.4 per cent attend modern or technical schools.

Special: These schools have been created to serve the educational needs of those pupils who are unable to benefit from education in mainstream schools because of their particular needs. Each school usually serves the needs of one or two defined groups of children. For example, there are special schools serving the visually or hearing impaired or those whose behavioural problems are so severe as to make it impossible to educate them with their peers. There are 1,113 special schools in the maintained system in England.

Nursery: In the maintained sector these schools provide education for children between three and five years. The majority of children attending such schools do so on a part-time basis. They are staffed by teachers specially trained for the needs of this age group and by qualified nursery nurses. There are 508 nursery schools in the maintained system in England attended by 45,157 children. In the private sector there are nursery schools which may have the same level of staff qualification, but there are also some which are staffed and function in the same way as playgroups. There are no adequate statistics available for the numbers of private nursery schools. Nursery classes attached to infant, first or primary schools have the same staffing rules as nursery schools.

Infant: All children must attend school from the beginning of the school term after their fifth birthday, although many will start earlier than this. Unless they enter a nursery school or class, their first experience of formal schooling will be in an infant school or class. Infant schools usually provide education for children from five to seven years. Within the legislation on curriculum issues this age group is known as Key Stage 1. This stage of learning lays the foundations for everything that follows.

Junior: These schools provide education for children between seven and eleven years. For most children this will be the period during which they acquire many of the skills that enable them to face future learning with confidence. They will also begin to develop a wide range of interests. For some children these interests will form the basis for a future career or hobby. Within the legislation on curriculum issues this age group is known as Key Stage 2.

Primary: Schools that combine the infant and junior age ranges are referred to as primary schools. In some small primary schools there will be no clear division between the infant and junior stages; indeed there may well be a class that contains children from both key stages. When the education of children under eleven years is being discussed it is often referred to as the primary phase of education. There are 18,069 primary schools in England, including all separate infant and junior schools.

First: In some LEAs the ages at which children transfer from one school to another vary from the pattern in the majority. As the name First School implies these schools provide education for children between the age of five, when they enter school, and either eight or nine, depending on the pattern of organization adopted in the particular education authority.

Middle: These schools usually provide education either from the age of eight to twelve or from nine to thirteen years depending on the pattern of organization adopted in the education authority. For administrative reasons, some authorities have adjusted the age groups in recent years. It is important to check the age range served by middle schools in each different authority where they exist. Middle schools that cater for children up to twelve years are regarded as primary schools. Those serving children up to thirteen years old are regarded as secondary schools.

Secondary: These schools may serve pupils from 11 years to 18, although some may serve a smaller age group depending on local circumstances. The years from 11 to 14 are known in curriculum legislation as Key Stage 3 and between 14 and 16 as Key Stage 4.

High: This name is often given to secondary schools that draw from middle schools and whose intake is, therefore, either twelve or thirteen years old on entry to the school. Sometimes the name is also used to describe a secondary school. Junior High school is sometimes used to describe a school serving Key Stage 3 only.

Sixth-form college: In some areas pupils transfer from secondary school at the age of sixteen to a central college catering for the needs of students between the ages of 16 and 19. Where such colleges offer principally a pattern of academic courses, they are known as sixth-form colleges. Where they offer a wider range of courses they may be called further education colleges or tertiary colleges. All these colleges form a separate sector of education whose funding comes direct from central Government sources through the Learning and Skills Councils. In a few areas where there are sixth-form colleges, some secondary schools have retained their sixth forms and hence provide a range of choices for pupils at this age.

Religious character: Schools that have been founded by a faith group or a denomination within a faith are designated by The Department for Education and Skills as having a 'religious character'. These schools may be 'voluntary' or 'foundation' schools but cannot be 'community' schools.

Joint: These are voluntary schools where more than one religious denomination is represented on the trust of the school. There are joint Anglican/ Roman Catholic schools and joint Anglican/ Methodist schools. The interest in these schools has been growing as part of the ecumenical movement.

Secular: This is sometimes used to describe community schools and those which do not have a 'religious character'.

b. The independent system

This includes all schools to which parents, or someone on their behalf, pay fees for their children's education. There are 2,188 independent schools in England providing education for 569,253 pupils.

Public: These schools are usually affiliated to the Headmasters' and Headmistresses' Conference or the equivalent organizations for girls' schools. They include many of the oldest and most famous schools in the country. All these schools are in the private sector of education. They are usually owned by charitable trusts. Most public schools admit pupils at either 11 or 13 years and also to the sixth form. Some have preparatory departments.

Private: These are the schools in the independent sector of education which are not in the Headmasters' and Headmistresses' Conference. While some are owned by charitable trusts others may be owned by private proprietors. Some schools in this part of education may be catering for children with special education needs.

Preparatory: Traditionally most of the larger public schools have accepted pupils at the age of thirteen. Preparatory schools provide education up to this age and specialize in preparing pupils for the entrance examinations of the schools serving the older age groups. Some, but not all, such schools are linked to a specific senior school.

Special: Some schools in the private sector serve pupils with special educational needs. They may often accept placement of pupils in their school from LEAs who pay the fees. In some schools such pupils will be in the majority. There are 4,653 pupils in independent special schools.

Religious: Within the independent sector it is difficult to identify all the schools which have a strong religious commitment. Some have been founded to provide an education that reflects a particular religion or denomination. Such schools would be expected to make that identity clear and to have some form of chaplaincy or its equivalent in place for the school. Other schools may have developed a religious identity as a result of the work of religiously committed teachers or governors.

Secular: Those schools that have no clearly identified religious commitment could be referred to as secular.

Nursery/kindergarten/playgroup: There are a number of private nursery schools, kindergartens and playgroups providing an educational experience for children under statutory school age. There is no clear description of each type and all should be subject to inspection by the Local Authority Social Services department to ensure that the premises and other arrangements are appropriate for the age group. Playgroups tend to have high levels of parental involvement in their day-to-day activities. Some private Nursery schools may require very little time commitment from parents. Naturally, the contribution that parents are asked to pay towards the cost reflects the ratio of paid staff to children and the support in kind or time that parents are asked to make. In some areas the Social Services department may actively support some nursery provision by providing grants or meeting the cost of a proportion of places that are then free to children.

Members of Churches Together in Britain and Ireland

The Baptist Union of Great Britain
Cherubim and Seraphim Council of Churches
The Church in Wales
The Church of England
The Church of Ireland
The Church of Scotland
Congregational Federation
The Council of African and Caribbean Churches
The Council of Oriental Orthodox Christian Churches
Evangelische Synode Deutscher Sprache in Grossbritannien (Synod of German-speaking Churches)
Free Churches' Group of Churches Together in England
Greek Orthodox Church
Oecumenical Patriarchate (Archdiocese of Thyateria and Great Britain)
Independent Methodist Churches
International Ministerial Council of Great Britain
Joint Council of Afro-Caribbean Churches
Light and Life Mission
Lutheran Council of Great Britain
Methodist Church
Methodist Church in Ireland
Moravian Church
New Testament Assembly
Presbyterian Church of Wales
Religious Society of Friends
Roman Catholic Church in England and Wales
Roman Catholic Church in Scotland
Russian Orthodox Church
Salvation Army (British Territory)
Scottish Episcopal Church
Serbian Orthodox Church
Undeb Yr Annibynwyr Cymraeg (Union of Welsh Independents)
United Free Church of Scotland

United Reformed Church
Wesleyan Holiness Church

Associate Members
Roman Catholic Church in Ireland
Seventh Day Adventist Church

List of Diocesan Board of Education offices

Bath and Wells
Director of Education
Diocesan Education Office
The Old Deanery
Wells, BA5 2UG
Tel: 01749 670777
email: education@bathwells.anglican.org

Birmingham
Director of Education
Diocesan Education Office
Church House
175 Harborne Park Road
Birmingham, B17 0BH
Tel: 0121 426 0417
email:m.edwards@birmingham.anglican.org

Blackburn
Director of Education
Diocesan Education Office
Cathedral Close
Blackburn, BB1 5AA
Tel: 01254 544421
email: peter.ballard@blackburn.anglican.org

Bradford
Director of Education
Diocesan Education Office
Cathedral Hall
Stott Hill
Bradford, BD1 4ET
Tel: 01274 725958
email: rachel-education@bradford.u-net.com

Bristol
Director of Education
Diocesan Education Office
All Saints RE Centre
1 All Saints Court
Bristol, BS1 1JN
Tel: 0117 927 7454
email: allsaints@bristoldiocese.org

Canterbury
Director of Education
Diocesan Education Office
Lady Wootton's Green
Canterbury, CT1 1NQ
Tel: 01227 459401
email: rbristow@diocant.org

Carlisle
Director of Education
Diocesan Education Office
Church Centre
West Walls
Carlisle, CA3 8UE
Tel: 01228 538086
email: dir-educ@carlisle-c-of-e.org

Chelmsford
Director of Education
Diocesan Education Office
53 New Street
Chelmsford, CM1 1AT
Tel: 01245 294440
email: hartleyp@chelmsford.anglican.org

Chester

Director of Education
Diocesan Education Office
Church House
Lower Lane
Aldford
Chester, CH3 6HP
Tel: 01244 620444
email: chesterDBE@dial.pipex.com

Chichester

Director of Education
Diocesan Education Office
211 New Church Road
Hove, BN3 4ED
Tel: 01273 421021
email: jeremy.taylor@diochi.org.uk

Coventry

Director of Education
Diocesan Education Office
Church House
Palmerston Road
Coventry, CV5 6FJ
Tel: 024 7667 3467
email: linda.dbe@covdioc.org

Derby

Director of Education
Diocesan Education Office
Church House, Full Street
Derby, DE1 3DR
Tel: 01332 382233
email: david@ddbe.freeserve.co.uk

Durham

Director of Education
Diocesan Education Office
Carter House
Pelaw Leazes Lane
Durham, DH1 1TB
Tel: 0191 374 6005
email: David.Whittington@durham.anglican.org

Ely

Director of Education
Diocesan Office
Bishop Woodford House
Barton Road
Ely, CB7 4DX
Tel: 01353 663579
email: ed&t@office.ely.anglican.org

Exeter

Director of Education
Diocesan Education Office
Renslade House
Bonhay Road
Exeter, EX4 3AY
Tel: 01392 432149
email: dde@exeter.anglican.org

Gloucester

Director of Education
Diocesan Education Office
4 College Green
Gloucester, GL1 2LB
Tel: 01452 410022
email: pmetcalf@glosdioc.org.uk

Guildford

Director of Education
Education Centre
The Cathedral
Guildford, GU2 7UP
Tel: 01483 450423
email: derek.holbird@cofeguildford.org.uk

Hereford

Director of Education
Diocesan Office
The Palace
Hereford, HR4 9BL
Tel: 01432 357864
email: education@diooffice.freeserve.co.uk

Leicester

Director of Education
Diocesan Education Office
Church House
3/5 St Martin's East
Leicester, LE1 5FX
Tel: 0116 248 7450
email: ptaylor@chouse.leicester.anglican.org

Lichfield

Director of Education
Diocesan Education Centre
St Mary's House, The Close
Lichfield, WS13 7LD
Tel:01423 869839
email: peter.lister@lichfield.anglican.org

Lincoln

Director of Education
Diocesan Education Centre
Church House
Lincoln, LN2 1PU
Tel: 01522 569600
email: lincolndio@claranet.co.uk

Liverpool

Director of Education
Diocesan Education Centre
Church House, 1 Hanover Street
Liverpool, L1 3DW
Tel: 0151 709 9722
email:jon.liv.dbe@ukgateway.net

London

Director of Education
London Diocesan House
36 Causton Street
Tel: 020 7932 1157
email: tom.peryer@dlondon.org.uk

Manchester

Director of Education
5th Floor, Diocesan Church House
90 Deansgate
Manchester, M3 2GJ
Tel: 0161 834 1022
email: jainsworth@manchester.anglican.org

Newcastle

Director of Education
Diocesan Education Office
Church House
St John's Terrace
North Shields, NE29 6HS
Tel: 0191 270 4141
email: m.nicholson@newcastle.anglican.org

Norwich

Director of Education
Diocesan House
109 Dereham Road
Easton
Norwich, Norfolk
NR9 5ES
Tel: 01603 881352
email: CynthiaWake@norwich.anglican.org

Oxford

Director of Education
Diocesan Church House
North Hinksey
Oxford, OX2 0NB
Tel: 01865 208236
email: schools@dch.oxford.anglican.org.uk

Peterborough

Director of Education
Education Department
Bouverie Court
The Lakes
Northampton, NN4 7YD
Tel: 01604 887006
email:stephen.partridge@peterborough-
diocese.org.uk

Portsmouth

Director of Education
Diocesan Education Office
Cathedral House
St Thomas Street
Portsmouth, PO1 2HA
Tel: 023 9282 2053
email: dde@portsmouth.anglican.org

Ripon and Leeds

Director of Education
The Castle CE School
Stockwell Road
Knaresborough, HG5 0JN
Tel: 01543 306040
email: janmack.riponleeds@lineone.net

Rochester

Director of Education
Education Office
Deanery Gate
The Precinct
Rochester, Kent
ME1 1SJ
Tel: 01634 843667
email: education@rochester.anglican.org

St Albans

Director of Education
Diocesan education Centre
Hall Grove
Welwyn Garden City
AL7 4PJ
Tel: 01707 332321/2
email: education@stalbansdioc.org.uk

St Edmundsbury and Ipswich

Director of Education
Churchgates House
Cutler Street
Ipswich, IP1 1UQ
Tel: 01473 298560
email: david@stedmundsbury.anglican.org

Salisbury

Director of Education
Diocesan Education Centre
Audley House, Crane Street
Salisbury, SP1 2QA
Tel: 01722 411977
email: jo.little@salisbury.anglican.org

Sheffield

Director of Education
Diocesan Church House
Sheffield Diocese
95–99 Effingham Street
Rotherham. S65 1BL
Tel: 01709 512446
email: malcolm.robertson@sheffield-diocese.org.uk

Sodor and Man

Sodor and Man Diocesan Office
Holly Cottage
Ballaughton Meadows
Douglas
Isle of Man, IM2 1JG

Southwark

Director of Education
Diocesan Education Office
Southwark Diocese
48 Union Street
London, SE1 1TD
Tel: 020 7234 9200
email: linda.borthwick@dswark.org.uk

Southwell

Director of Education
Diocesan Education Office
Dunham House, Westgate
Southwell, NG25 0JL
Tel:01636 814504
email:education@southwell.anglican.org

Truro

Director of Education
Diocesan Education Office
Diocesan House
Kenwyn
Truro, TR1 3JQ
Tel: 01872 274352
email: julianp.trurodio@virgin.net

Wakefield

Director of Education
Diocesan Education Office
Church House
1 South Parade
Wakefield, WF1 1LP
Tel: 01924 371802
email:barbara.wright@wakefield.anglican.org

Winchester

Director of Education
Diocesan Education Office
Church House
9 The Close
Winchester, SO23 9LS
Tel: 01962 624767
email: richard.lindley@chsewinchester.clara.net

Worcester

Director of Education
Diocesan Education Office
The Old Palace
Deansway
Worcester, WR1 2JE
Tel: 01905 732825
email: dmorphy@cofe-worcester.org.uk

York

Director of Education
Diocesan Board of Education
Diocesan House
Aviator Court
Clifton Moor
York, YO30 4JW
Tel: 01904 699512
email: acm@yorkdbe.demon.co.uk

List of *RE* centres

Banbury RE Centre

C/o The Methodist Church
Marlborough Road
Banbury, OX16 8BZ
Tel: 01295 262676

The BFSS National RE Centre

Brunel University College
Osterley Campus
Borough Road
Isleworth, TW7 5DU
Tel: 020 8891 0121 (ext. 2656)

Bradford Interfaith Education Centre

Listerhills Road
Bradford
West Yorks, BD7 1HD
Tel: 01274 731674

Bristol Methodist District Resource Centre

Wesley College
College Drive
Henbury Road
Bristol, BS10 7QD
Tel: 0117 959 1200

Croydon RE Resource Centre

The Crescent
Croydon, CR0 2HN
Tel: 020 8689 5343

Hants Inspection & Advisory Service

County RE Centre
Falcon House
Romsey Road
Winchester, SO22 5PL
Tel: 01962 863134

Jewish Resource Centre

CREDE
Howard Building
Room 102, Roehampton Institute
Digby Stuart College
Roehampton Lane
London, SW15 5PH
Tel: 020 8392 3349

Keswick Hall RE Centre

University of East Anglia
Norwich, NR4 7TH
Tel: 01603 505975

The National Society's RE Centre

Church House
Great Smith Street
London
SW1P 3NZ
Tel: 020 7898 1495

North East London RE Centre

Marshall Hall
Eric Road
Chadwell Heath
Romford, RM6 6JH
Tel: 020 8590 5331

Slough RS Centre

Slough Education Centre
Queens Road
Slough, Berks
SL1 3QW
Tel: 01753 577466

Southampton RE Centre

38/39 St. Mary's Street
Southampton
SO14 1NR
Tel: 01703 228480

South Essex RE Centre

St Barnabas Church
Woodfield Road
Hadleigh, SS7 2EJ
Tel: 01702 552099

South London Multifaith Centre

Lewisham Professional Development
Centre
Kilmorie Road
London, SE23 2SP
Tel: 020 8291 5005

Welsh National Centre for RE

School of Education, UCNW
Ffordd Deiniol
Bangor
Gwynedd, LL57 2UW
Tel: 01248 382956

The Westhill RE Centre

Westhill College
Selly Oak
Birmingham, B29 6LL
Tel: 0121 472 7248

The York RE Centre

Lord Mayor's Walk
York, YO3 7EX
Tel: 01904 612512

List of Church colleges of higher education

The Principal
Bishop Grosseteste College
Lincoln, LN1 3DY
Tel: 01522 529347
email: registry@bgc.ac.uk

The Principal
Canterbury Christ Church
University College
North Holmes Road
Canterbury, CT1 1QU
Tel: 01227 76770
email: m.wright@cant.ac.uk

The Principal
Chester College of HE
Park Gate Road
Chester, CH1 4BJ
Tel: 01244 375444
email: t.wheeler@chester.ac.uk

The Principal
College of St Mark & St John
Derriford Road
Plymouth, PL6 8BH
Tel: 01752 636829
email: pains@marjon.ac.uk

The Principal
King Alfred's College
Winchester, SO22 4NR
Tel: 01962 82722
email: c.mackensie@wkac.ac.uk

The Principal
Liverpool Hope College
Hope Park
Liverpool, L16 9JD
Tel: 0151 291 3243
email: lees@livhope.ac.uk

The Principal
St Martin's College
Bowerham
Lancaster, LA1 3JD
Tel: 01524 384562/1
email: c.j.carr@ucsm.ac.uk

The Principal
Trinity College
Carmarthen
Dyfed, SA31 3EP
Tel: 01267 676767
email: m.r.williams@trinity-cm.ac.uk

The Principal
University College
Bishop Otter Campus
College Lane
Chichester, PO19 4PE
Tel: 01243 816051
email: i.cherrett@chihe.ac.uk

The Director
The University of Gloucestershire
PO Box 220
The Park Campus
Cheltenham, GL50 2QF
Tel: 01242 532701
email: admissions@chelt.ac.uk

The Principal
Whitelands College
West Hill
London, SW15 3SN
Tel: 020 8392 3000
email: d.peacock@roehampton.ac.uk

The Principal
York St John
Lord Mayor's Walk
York, YO3 7EX
Tel: 01904 716601
email: d.willcocks@ucrysj.ac.uk

Other organizations

Church Pastoral Aid Society (CPAS)
Athena Drive
Tachbrook Park
Warwick, CV34 6NG
Tel: 01926 458458
email: info@cpas.org.uk

The National Society for Promoting Religious Education
Church House
Great Smith Street
London, SW1P 3NZ
Tel: 020 7898 1497

Scripture Union
207–209 Queensway
Bletchley
Milton Keynes, MK2 2EB
Tel: 0908 856000
email: postmaster@scriptureunion.org.uk

United Society for the Propagation of the Gospel (USPG)
Partnership House
157 Waterloo Road
London, SE1 8XA
Tel: 020 7928 8681
email: enquiries@uspg.org.uk

Notes

Extracts from *The Way ahead* report appear at the beginning of each chapter.
The bibliographic information is given in Note 1 only and in the reference section.

1   *The Way ahead: Church of England schools in the new millennium,* Church House
Publishing, 2001.

2   The word 'teacher' is used throughout this section but many of the comments
and suggestions are just as appropriate to others working in school contexts and
to school governors.

3   Before 1/4/02 this was 15 per cent of all improvements and external repairs.

4   *Welcoming Schools,* Penarth, Church in Wales, 1994.

5   *Reaching Children,* Diocese of Norwich, 2001.

6   All the statistics in this section refer to January 2001 figures and are reported
in terms of full-time equivalents. The number of governors is estimated from the
number of schools.

References

Anonymous, *Welcoming Schools*, Church in Wales, 1994.

The Alternative Service Book 1980, Clowes/SPCK/Cambridge University Press, 1980.

Bailey, J., *Worship!*, National Society/Church House Publishing, 1999.

Barton, D., Brown, A. and Brown, E., *Open the Door*, National Society/Oxford Diocesan Education Services, 1994.

Brown, A. *Christianity in the Agreed Syllabus*, National Society, 1994.

Brown, A. and Lankshear, D. W. *Inspection Handbook for Section 23 Inspections in Schools of the Church of England and Church in Wales*, National Society, 2000.

Brown, A. and Seaman, A., *Feeding Minds and Touching Hearts*, National Society/Church House Publishing, 2001.

Church Schools Review Group, *The Way Ahead: Church of England Schools in the New Millennium*, Church House Publishing, 2001.

Common Worship: Services and Prayers for the Church of England, Church House Publishing, 2000

Dearing, R., *The National Curriculum and Its Assessment*, School Curriculum and Assessment Authority, 1993.

Duffy, W., *Children and Bereavement*, National Society/Church House Publishing, 1995.

Excellence in Schools, HMSO, 2001

Foster, David (ed.), 'Prayers for Young People', *The Catholic Prayerbook from Downside Abbey*, T & T Clark, 1999.

Francis, L. J., *Partnership in Rural education*, Collins, 1987a.

Francis, L. J., *Religion in the Primary School*, Collins Liturgical, 1987b.

Francis, L. J. and Lankshear, D. W., 'The relationship between Church Schools and Local Church Life: distinguishing between aided and controlled schools', *Educational Studies*, Vol. 27, No. 4, pp. 425–38, 2001.

Francis, L. J. and Lankshear, D. W., *Christian perspectives on Church Schools*, Gracewing – Fowler/Wright, 1993.

Francis, L. J. and Lankshear, D. W., in *Children in the Way*, National Society/Church House Publishing, 1988.

Her Majesty's Chief Inspector of Schools, *Guidance on the Inspection of Nursery and Primary Schools*, 1995.

Herbert, Christopher, (compiler) *Pocket Prayers*, National Society/Church House Publishing, 1993a.

Herbert, Christopher, (compiler), *Prayers for Children*, National Society/Church House Publishing, 1993b.

Lankshear, D. W., *Governing and Managing Church Schools*, National Society/Church House Publishing, 2000.

Lankshear, D. W., *Pocket Prayers for Teachers*, National Society/Church House Publishing, 2002.

Patterns for Worship, Church House Publishing, 1995.

Raising Achievement in Our Schools: Model of Effective Teaching, Hay McBer, 2000.

Reaching Children, Diocese of Norwich, 2001.